MANSKILLS

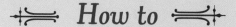

How to

Avoid Embarrassing Yourself

AND Impress Everyone Else

Creative Publishing
international

Creative Publishing international

Copyright © 2011
Creative Publishing international, Inc.
400 First Avenue North, Suite 400
Minneapolis, Minnesota 55401
1-800-328-0590
www.creativepub.com

Printed in China

10 9 8 7 6

Library of Congress Cataloging-in-Publication Data

Peterson, Chris
 Manskills : how to avoid embarrassing yourself and impress everyone else / by Chris Peterson.
  p. cm.
 Summary: "Everything a man needs to know in today's world, including tips on home repair, car repair, electronics, cleaning, personal grooming, fine dining, traveling, etiquette, outdoor skills and the fine art of conversation"--Provided by publisher.
 ISBN-13: 978-1-58923-631-8 (soft cover)
 ISBN-10: 1-58923-631-9 (soft cover)
 1. Home economics. I. Title.
TX295.P48 2011
640--dc22

2011009687

President/CEO: Ken Fund
Group Publisher: Bryan Trandem

Home Improvement Group

Associate Publisher: Mark Johanson
Managing Editor: Tracy Stanley
Creative Director: Michele Lanci-Altomare
Art Direction/Design: Brad Springer,
    Kim Winscher, James Kegley
Production Managers: Laura Hokkanen,
Linda Halls

Author: Chris Peterson
Page Layout Artist: Heather Parlato
Illustrator: Jason Colehour
Proofreader: Ingrid Sundstrom Lundegaard

Table of Contents

MAN. THE NOBLE ANIMAL. WELL, KIND OF. MEN HAVE thumbs and we walk upright, which helps us stand out in the animal kingdom. But it's these things we can do, our own unique skills that make us special. Not just any skills. Certain skills define a man, make him the pride of his pride, the envy of others, the . . . well you get the picture.

We call those particular skills Manskills, and they are captured handily and succinctly in this book.

These are the proficiencies that all great males must have. If there were an SAT for manhood, these would be on it. They lie beyond the simple

tricks and stunts that sometimes pass for manliness: burping the alphabet, burning rubber from a dead stop, deciphering box scores. Sure, all those are very useful. Very useful.

But if you want to be a real man, admired by peers, desired by women, and generally carried on the shoulders of the world, you must master Manskills. Like Luke mastered Jedi mind tricks. Just like that.

Many of these may already be second nature to you. As king of your own little castle, you may have already mastered the plumbing arts and know everything there is to know about how to unstick a door without the aid of small explosives. You may be a pro behind the wheel, able to slip away from that black sedan that has been tailing you like so much smoke in the wind.

But Manskills is about the total picture, the total man. It's about everything you should know to be a complete and thoroughly alpha male. And why would you ever want to be anything but the complete man. After all, you wouldn't go out of the house with half a shirt on, would you? Okay, maybe you would, but the point is that you should never sally forth as anything but a fully, 100-percent skilled hombre.

You see, the man who has mastered ManSkills has mastered his own fate, owns his destiny. He is the man of the beer commercial and the Arrow Shirt ad. He is confident, and a winner, and in control. He is the prince among lesser men, the captain of the ship, the . . . well you get the picture.

So the question is not whether you master ManSkills. No. That is not the question. The question is: What the heck are you waiting for, Bumble?

We've set you up, put all the skills in neat little categories, thrown in some instructive illustrations, and covered all the bases. Now, dear friend, it's up to you. Time to turn the page, learn the skills, and claim the badge of manskillfulness!

CHAPTER № 1

Shelter Savvy

FIRST THERE WAS THE CAVE. BUT THE CAVE LEAKED, and there was graffiti on the walls, and the plumbing sucked, and there was no door to hide behind so the sabertooth tiger used the cave as his personal pantry.

So man invented rudimentary tools, and then there was the hut. The hut was nice, but the roof leaked, the placed smelled of mud and decay, mice nested in the walls, and the dirt floor was, well, dirt. Woman complained until man couldn't take it anymore.

So then there was the house. Solid roof, nice wood floor, and no sabertooth tigers. One bronze age, one Iron Age and one industrial revolution later and, ta da, lots of tools for the house. Given that the great law of houses is that, left to their own devices, they crumble, there are many uses for the tools. And then there are new tools. And more uses. It's a wonderful hardware store-sponsored circle of life. All of which is why, as part of a complete repertoire of Manskills, you must master both the tools and techniques that will keep the house together.

Luckily, this is often fun. It's the jaded man who doesn't enjoy an afternoon spent destroying a hard surface with a jackhammer. And few feelings can rival the satisfaction of a perfectly straight painted line that exactly separates trim from wall. And that's to say nothing of simple self-preservation of quieting that running toilet that is messing with your sleep. Yes, there are many rewards to mastering the plentitude of home skills.

Should you ever grow weary of exercising those skills, the raw mechanical abilities it takes to make your home a castle, just think what it would be like to battle sabertooth tigers when mowing the lawn. Things could be much, much worse, chum.

Stop a Handsaw from Binding

The most basic of Manskills is handling a handsaw. It starts with knowing which kind of saw you should use, rip or crosscut. Pretty simple really: if you need to cut across the grain you use—wait for it—a crosscut saw. If you're cutting parallel to the grain, use a ripsaw. Regardless of which type you're using, both can bind when the kerf (the gap of your cutline) closes down, cinching the blade. It's a frustrating experience and it can lead to sawing off line (not to mention a whole lot of words the kids shouldn't be hearing).

Prevent binding by keeping saws sharp and in good condition. When sawing, use a spacer such as a thin piece of scrap, an awl, or a nail to keep the kerf open. Just stick the spacer in the kerf behind the saw, as you saw along the cut line.

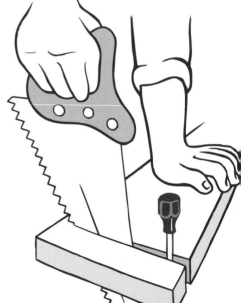

Remove a Stripped Screw

A stripped screw has to rank in the top three among the all-time great frustrations of any do-it-yourselfer. Getting that bothersome fastener out of its hole is like a lot of life: you can do it the easy way or the hard way. If the screw is just slightly stripped, stop before you do any further damage and use the easy way. Press a piece of rubber gasket or a rubber band down over the screw head, and then press down hard with the screwdriver, jamming the blade into what's left of the screw-head channels. The rubber often creates enough tension in the stripped head to hold onto the blade of the screwdriver so that the screw can be slowly removed.

However, if you've let your frustration get the better of you and you really stripped that sucker out, time to do things the hard way. Buy a screw extractor (or better yet, a set) of the smallest size that comes closest to matching the screw size. Drill a pilot hole in the center of the stripped screw head using a bit that is at least a size smaller than the screw. Now use a hammer to tap the point of the extractor into the pilot hole. Attach the T handle onto the square shank of the extractor (or use vise grip pliers if your forgot to buy the T handle) and start slowly turning the extractor counterclockwise. With a little bit of patience, you'll have an empty screw hole in no time.

If it's the screw hole that stripped, you'll need a slightly different solution. Basically, you want to create friction where there is none. Wrap the screw in unstripped electrical wire (speaker wire will work as well) counterclockwise. Then screw it in slowly and the threads should bite securely into the surrounding surface.

Handle a Jackhammer

When your driveway starts looking like one of Baghdad's back roads, it needs replacing. You could do your time on the chain gang working the surface over with a sledgehammer and pick, but there's a better way. A situation like this is the perfect excuse to grab ahold of the ultimate macho tool—the jackhammer. Professionals use an air-powered model that requires a separate compressor. But you're not relocating a highway off-ramp; an electric model will supply all the breaking power you need for any surface you're likely to encounter around the house. For most jobs, you'll want a pointed or sharp spade bit. Use the thickest, shortest extension cord that provides adequate amps while still reaching everywhere you need to go. You'll also need to suit up. Jackhammering up a concrete slab is no job to skimp on safety gear. Wear boots, heavy gloves, thick pants, ear protection and a dust mask. Then go to town.

Hold the jackhammer at a slight angle leaning it against your upper thighs. Be patient and let the tool do the work; there's no need to push down on it. As you crack through the slab at a given point, lever under that section to lift it up a bit, making it easier to remove. Once you've broken up an area about a yard square, stop and remove the debris. (This gives both the tool and your body a chance to recuperate a little. You're not as young as you used to be.) Cut any rebar or mesh you encounter with a grinder or torch. Just make sure you stop at the slab that needs breaking up; jockeying that cement-smashing pogo stick can be addictive, and you just might find yourself thinking about how good a brand new sidewalk would look.

Replace a String Trimmer Spool

Nothing like getting ready to put the finishing touches on your newly mown lawn only to discover your power trimmer is out of cord. Time to reload that puppy and keep your grassy edges looking sharp.

Whenever you work on a power trimmer, make sure it's unplugged or that the spark plug wire on a gas model is disconnected; you still want to be able to count to ten after you're all done. Trimmers tend to be unwieldy, so replacing the spool will go a lot quicker if you work on a large flat surface (the garage floor will do if you don't have free space on your worktable). Some trimmers require that you replace the line with bulk cord, in which case just insert one end of the line through the spool's hole and hold it as you pull the rest of the line through the slot and wind the line in the direction of the arrow on the spool.

Higher-end models generally use replacement spools. Always check your manual; these instructions are for a Black-and-Decker model and yours might be slightly different. Press the release tabs on the spool hub cover and pull it off. Lift the spool out from the hub and clear any line or debris. Insert the end of the line on the new spool into the eyelet in the hub and pull the line through the hole, maintaining tension as you drop the new spool into place in the hub. The notched side should be exposed. Gently press the spool down and rotate it until you feel it drop into position. It should still be able to turn slightly to the left and right. Replace the hub cover and test on a patch of unruly grass to make sure you got it all right.

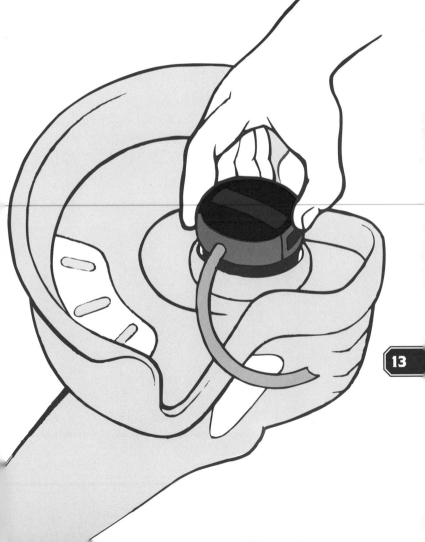

Use a Torque Wrench

The torque wrench is the forgotten soldier in the home craftsman's toolbox. Overtightening is one of the most common mistakes of the DIY guy changing his oil or cranking a new blade onto his edger. But this handy gadget is the cure for that disease, and it can spare you the frustration that accompanies a stripped bolt.

Do yourself a favor when buying a torque wrench and go for the more expensive ratchet style, rather than the simpler and less accurate needle-gauge type. Using the thing is pretty simple. Set the torque pounds on the wrench according to the recommendations of the car or tool manufacturer, and slowly tighten the nut. When you hit the target torque, the wrench will click or feel like it is slipping.

If you absolutely must go with a needle-gauge type, tighten the bolt steadily and slowly, until the needle pegs the number corresponding to the correct torque.

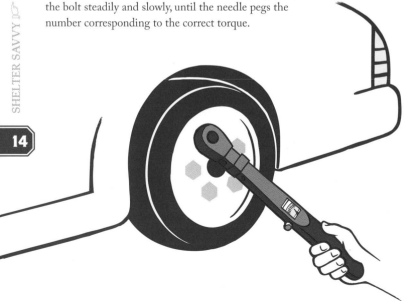

Stop a Toilet From Running

A toilet that won't stop running is a small thing that can become a big irritation in a quiet house. Turn off the waterworks by fixing the flapper valve that covers the drain hole in the bottom of your toilet tank. The "running" in the toilet is water flowing past the valve when it fails to completely close. This is usually caused by a blocked valve seat or a pull chain that is too short.

If you can't fix the problem by cleaning the valve seat or adjusting the chain, it's time for a new flapper valve. Replacements are available at hardware stores and are easy to install. First, turn off the water supply to the toilet at the shutoff valve. Remove the old valve by disconnecting the pull chain (note where on the length of chain the valve is hooked) and pulling it off the fill-tube mounting ears. Slip the new valve's tabs onto the ears and reconnect the chain. Then rest in peace.

Remove a Rusted Bolt

That engine block bolt won't come loose, so it's time to show it who's boss (and it ain't the bolt). Yeah, you could spray a penetrating product into the threads and wait around a few hours, but where's the fun in that? Turn to real-man remedies instead.

Heat the bolt with a small torch to expand the metal and break the rust bonds. Some brave souls hold a candle near the head so that the melted wax makes its way down into the threads, but the heat itself will likely work the magic.

No torch on hand? Turn to a tasty beverage. Create a dam around the bolt using plumber's putty or a similar material. Fill it with diet Coke and let it sit for about 20 minutes, until it seeps down into the threads. Give the bolt a sharp rap with a ballpeen hammer and it should come out easy as pie.

Drive a Nail with One Hand

Why does it always seem that you're just one hand short in the middle of every DIY project? You've got a nail in one hand, the hammer in the other, but how are you going to hold the boards together? Sure, you could use a nail gun, but there's a simpler solution: the one-handed nailing technique.

First, grasp a claw hammer from the side, in the same way you would grip the shifter ball handle in a '70 Hemi Cuda (yeah, you wish). Slide the head of the nail up between your index and middle fingers so that it's held securely, sticking out perpendicular to the side of the hammer. Now just drive the nail home with a solid swing of your arm. Put a little pepper on it and you'll drive it in far enough to hold it firm. Finish it off with a couple blows of the hammer and presto! Job done.

Repair a Leaking Pipe

Water squirting out a pipe in the basement can freak anyone out, so you can't blame her for wanting to call the plumber. Down deep somewhere that we don't discuss in bars, you too want to call a plumber. Fight the urge, brother, fight the urge.

Instead, show her your innovative handy side with a simple temporary fix that will stop the water flow until you can make a permanent repair. A small hole is no big deal if you can lay your hands on a couple of small hose clamps and a sheet of flat rubber gasket (you'll find both in abundant supply at the local hardware store). Cut the gasket so that it circles the pipe in a perfect sleeve. Then wrap it in position over the leak, and use the hose clamps on either end of the sleeve to create a snug patch. Add another clamp to apply pressure directly over the leak. Show her your handiwork because it ain't boasting if it's true. Leak? What leak?

Remove Gum from Carpeting

It's okay to vow revenge on whoever it was at your party who left that big hunk of Double Bubble in your retro orange shag carpet. This is not something friends do to friends and you shall have your revenge. But for now, concentrate on stopping that gum from becoming a bigger mess than it already is. The solution is as simple as a TV dinner: freeze it out. You can set a piece of ice right on the gum, but by the time the gum is frozen, you'll have a puddle to contend with. Do it the easier way by using a sports pack or a sandwich bag full of ice (you may have to replace it a couple of times until the gum is completely frozen). Once the gum is rock hard, just chip it out and go on the hunt for the criminal chewer.

Catch a Mouse

The only place mice are cute is at Disneyland. In your house, glue traps work great, but mice are notorious for avoiding them if others have already been trapped in the location. A more foolproof option (well, more creative anyway) involves a cardboard toilet-paper core, tape, and a large pail or kitchen garbage can.

Position the tube on the edge of a counter the mice frequent. Tape it down, so that an inch overlaps the counter edge and the rest sticks out over the floor. Slightly crease the underside of the tube at the edge of the counter. Center the pail under the tube's outer end and place a peanut butter-coated cracker just inside that end.

When the mouse takes the bait, the tube bends down and slides him into your trap. Then it's up to your conscience whether you free him in a local park, or flush him to a watery grave.

Patch Wallpaper Perfectly

Practicing your golf swing in the hall is never a good idea, especially when you wind up with a 2-inch gash in the wallpaper. Man up and make the repair with a scrap piece of wallpaper and a sharp razorblade. Tape the patch over the damaged section, aligning the pattern of the patch exactly with the pattern of the underlying wallpaper. Now use a sharp utility knife or razorblade to cut through both the patch and the bottom layer of wallpaper. Cut a square or rectangular shape, making sure to cut the patch large enough to completely cover the damaged area. Remove the taped sections of the patch, remove the damaged wallpaper section, and scrape out the underlying adhesive. Lay a new bed of adhesive, position the patch and roll it to remove any air bubbles. Now nobody will ever know how bad your swing really is.

Step 1

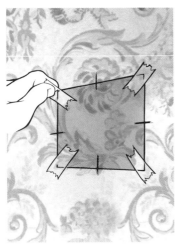

Step 2

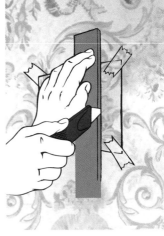

Patch a Metal Gutter

When the neighbors start openly gawking because there is more water pouring out of a hole in your metal gutter than is coming out of the downspout, it may well be time to take action. The damaged area needs to be free of rot before you patch it, so you don't have to redo the job anytime soon. The first step is to get up there when it's dry and scour the corroded area around the leak with a wire brush. Scrub thoroughly until you've exposed clean metal all around, then use tin snips to cut a sheet-metal patch slightly larger than the damaged area. Bend the patch to the shape of the gutter, matching the curve as closely as possible. Slather asphalt roofing cement on the back of the patch and set it into position in the gutter. Smooth the edges, and you're ready for the next storm.

Unstick a Wood Drawer

She loves that old wood dressing table she got from Aunt Edna, but the drawer that keeps sticking is an irritation every time she gets dressed. Be her hero by making that drawer glide open and closed like it was riding on air.

In some cases, the drawer will be warped slightly out of alignment. You can fix it by sanding the high points a little at a time until the drawer moves freely. (Follow up with the solution below, in any case.)

More likely, the wood is just old and misshapen from temperature changes and use, just rough enough to cause excess friction. Solve the problem with bar soap or a beeswax candle. Rub the soap or wax along the slide and surfaces where the drawer meets the desk's frame, applying a liberal coating. Pull the drawer in and out a few times and it should work like new.

Patch a Carpet

So you knocked a burning candle onto your brand new carpet? No problem. Damage such as cigarette burns are so common that some bright soul invented a round tool just for dealing with them, called a cookie cutter. Do yourself a favor and buy a metal or aluminum tool with detachable blades, rather than a plastic type.

Slip the blades into place, position the central pivot post in the center of the damage, and cut a circle down to the pad. Now cut a patch from a remnant or an inconspicuous area such as the back of a closet. Line the pad or subfloor with double-sided carpet tape and position the patch in place with the nap direction matching the existing carpet. Make the job even easier by buying a complete patch kit, including cutter, adhesive backing for the patch, and burlap undersurface to help hold the patch in place.

Straighten a Warped Door

We're all a little warped, but your doors shouldn't be. If you're having a problem with the door sticking or closing properly, check it top to bottom and on the diagonal with a straightedge, such as a long metal carpenter's level. When you detect a noticeable warp in a door, remove it from its hinges and set it across two sawhorses with the crest of the warp facing up. Then place several weights on top of the warp. Use those barbell weights that never seem to move from the floor of the garage; cinder blocks work just as well. The greater the weight, the quicker the fix, but don't overload the door to the point of cracking. Place a clean, thick towel underneath the weights to protect the door's surface. Keep checking the door with a level until it is completely straight, and then reinstall it. (Be patient; this usually takes days.)

23

Fix a Sticking Door Lock

Ten minutes spent trying to get your key to work in your door lock is time you could spend much more productively (watching Ultimate Fighting Championship, for instance). Fix the problem for good. The first thing to consider is how cold it is outside. Exterior door locks can freeze just like car locks, and simply heating it up or applying de-icer may be the solution.

More likely though, the lock mechanism is clogged with dirt. Before you spring for a whole new lockset, wash the lock out with a little WD-40 and blast it out with a few quick blasts from a can of air. Keep a rag around the straw on the canned air, to seal the lock opening and stop vaporized lubricant and dirt from blowing back out all over your clothes. Finish up with a dose of graphite lubricant and the key should turn the lock freely.

Straighten a Sliding Door Track

A sliding glass door shouldn't take Superman strength to open. It may be a good workout, but you need to put the slide back in that sliding door. The first step is to thoroughly clean out the track and the door's wheels (this may mean removing the door from the track, but bite the bullet and do it). Lubricate both the wheels and track with silicone lubricant.

If the door still moves reluctantly, the track's guides are probably out of alignment. Raised sliding door tracks take a beating from foot traffic and just regular wear and tear. Reverse all that by using a scrap piece of wood (or even the right thickness of hardbound book will do) that fits snugly as a tapping block inside the channel. Position the block in place, and tap the outside wall of the track with a wooden mallet to realign the track guides.

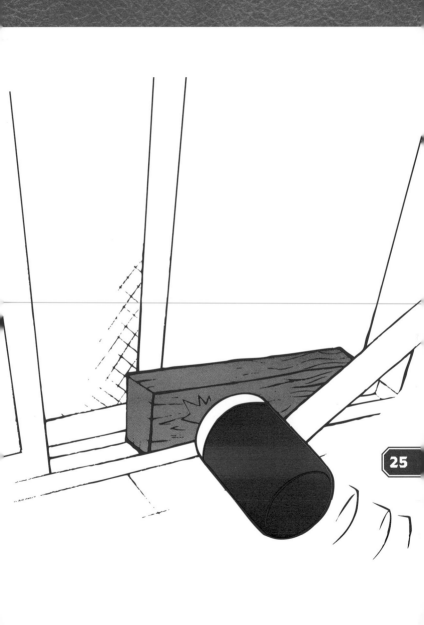

Snake a Clog

There comes a time in every man's life when a big bottle of drain cleaner won't cut it. That's when you have to answer that fundamental question: Are you going to call a plumber, or will you affirm your manskillfulness and deal with that clog? If you're ready to take the bull by the horns, you need to lay your hands on a snake or, as it's called professionally, an auger. Rent large versions—including power snakes—or you can buy a more modest sized auger as a defense against inevitable future plumbing emergencies.

There are actually two types of augers, the "closet auger" that is used specifically for toilet clogs, and the drain auger that is used for all other clogs. A drain auger is generally the more useful purchase because it can be used for toilet clogs in a pinch.

To snake a clog, slip on some rubber gloves and guide the snake's corkscrew tip down the drain. Keep feeding the line into the drain, turning the handle counterclockwise as you do. Eventually, you'll feel the snake contact the clog.

When that happens, keeping turning the handle while pushing and pulling the line. This action often dislodges the material, which can be washed away with warm water. If the clog is a little more stubborn, start pulling pieces of it back up the pipe as you snake through the material, disposing of it as you do. This can get messy, but suppress your gag response, get a bucket and clear out all the material. Then flush the drainpipe thoroughly.

Keep pipes clog-free by dumping a half-cup of baking soda down the drain, rinsing with just enough cold water to carry the baking soda down into the pipes. Then pour a kettleful of boiling water down the drain.

Free a Stuck Double-Hung Window

Don't go all Jean-Claude Van Damme on that window; there are many easier ways to get it to open, and breaking the glass is only going to add to your problems. Older double-hung windows tend to stick for two reasons: they have been painted shut or they have swelled with moisture. In either case, you want to fix the immediate problem so that you can get fresh air moving through the room. Then you want to take steps to make sure the window doesn't get stuck again.

If the weather is humid and you suspect moisture is the villain, heat the window with a paint-stripping gun set on low. Hold it farther than normal from the surface and move it rapidly over the area (you aren't looking to strip the paint, just get rid of excess moisture). You can also use a hairdryer set on medium or high. In either case, constantly move the jet of hot air to prevent bubbling of the paint.

More often, paint build-up is the culprit. This is such a common problem that there's a special tool called a window zipper tool to fix it. This handy item features a thin, heart-shaped blade with rows of teeth, mounted on the end of a wood handle. You stick it into the gap between the sash and the side jamb and slide the blade up and down. A few passes should clean the offending paint out enough for the window to slide free. If you can't find a window zipper tool (local hardware stores are more likely to carry them than large home centers) a putty knife is a decent substitute.

Once you've freed the window, lubricate the channel with a little paraffin wax (the easiest way is to just rub a candle onto the wooden guides).

Cut in Paint Like a Pro

Few things spruce up your interior quite like a finely detailed paint job. But the icing on that particular cake is the line you lay between different surfaces and different paint colors. It's one of the fine points that separates the manskilled master of his castle from the unskilled DIY rookie. Whether you're painting around the trim on windows or painting the walls a different color from the ceiling, how well you "cut in" will determine how crisp the result looks. Be about the crisp, dude.

Many do-it-yourselfers are intimidated by the idea of laying a straight line of paint freehand, especially when there are a ton of devices on the market that claim to help you do just that. But cutting in freehand like a pro only takes a little practice and patience. And it should be telling that you'll never catch a pro using a special pad or latest gimmick "as seen on TV."

Many people find it helpful to use an angled sash brush, but regardless of the cut of brush, pick a high-quality 2½-inch brush for cutting-in duty. Load the tips of the brush with a modest amount of paint (remember: you can always go back over what you've done), and press the brush against the surface so that it fans out slightly. Now drag it along so that one edge defines the line along the surface that you're cutting in against. You should only be able to go a few inches before the brush runs out of paint. (Remember that part about "patience"?) Reload the brush and continue the line. The key is breathing evenly and trusting your hand. It's like using that universal remote for the first time; the more practice you get under your belt, the faster and more confident you'll be.

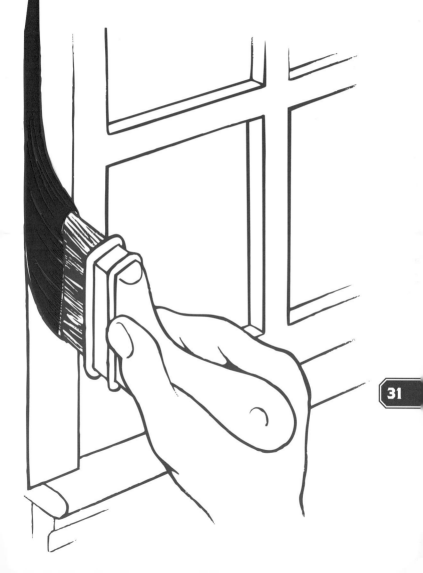

Cut Glass

Once upon time, the ability to cut glass was one of the essential aptitudes of a self-respecting man. These days, it's a little bit of a lost art. But you can resurrect it to replace broken glass lickety split.

You'll usually be cutting a piece to replace a broken pane in an older single-glazed window. Measuring is crucial, so that you leave about ⅛ inch between the pane edges and the sash, for expansion and contraction. Measure twice and get down to slicing the glass to fit.

Work on a clean, level surface. Place the glass on a rubber mat or other material that will stop it from sliding. Clean the face you're going to cut, and measure and mark the cut line. Use a straightedge with a cork or rubber backing, or tape it down. Be careful to position the straight edge so that the cutter's cutting wheel is exactly on top of the cut line.

Now gear up with a pair of safety glasses and gloves (at least when you snap the glass), and grasp the cutter as you would a pen, but at a severe angle, pressing down on the cutting wheel. Your index finger should be in position to guide the cut, but it should be far enough back of the head so that you can clearly see the cutting wheel at all times.

Now press down and pull the cutter toward you, using an even pressure all the way along the cut. Make the cut in one sure stroke. Hold the cut glass up so that you can clearly see the cut line, and use the ball on the back of the cutter to tap every inch or so along the line. Finally, position the glass so that the cut is aligned with the edge of the table, and lightly and quickly snap the waste piece off.

Replace a Furnace Filter

What if you could make all the air in the house cleaner, helping out any allergy sufferers that visit or live there (not to mention the rest of us who just want to breathe clean air)? And what if you could add months and maybe years to the life of your forced air furnace?

What if you could do both, with little time, money or effort? Well, man, you can. All it takes is changing your furnace filter on a regular basis. Furnace filters are so cheap and the job is so easy that there is just no reason not to do it. Just be sure to note the filter size before you hit the hardware store.

Most manufacturers recommend replacing the filter once a month, but no less than every three months. If you're like many homeowners, you may never have replaced yours. Shame on you. Go out and buy some filters—buy in bulk to save a considerable amount over the life of the furnace. Be ahead of the curve and mark the extra filters with the month they are to be installed, so you'll never have to try to figure out when you last replaced the filter.

To make the switch, turn off the furnace (always smart to trip the main breaker for safety's sake). Open the front of the furnace, which will usually entail removing a bottom or front access panel. You'll see the dirty filter mounted over the cold-air intake. Unclip it and slide it out. Then slide in the new filter, making sure the airflow arrows on the filter's frame or body point the right way, away from the cold air source.

Some systems come with a reusable filter (you'll know by the sturdy metal frame). Remove it as you would a replaceable unit, thoroughly rinse the screen with a hose, and let it dry before reinstalling. With a clean filter in place, everyone will breathe easier.

Chisel a Mortise

We all aspire to Norm Abrams-hood. If you hope of ever hitting that summit, you'll need to master that most basic of woodworking skills—chiseling a mortise.

Begin by marking the mortise with a pencil. Use a chisel that matches the mortise width, or you'll have to make two passes. Hold the chisel at a 45-degree angle, bevel side up, and tap it lightly with a hammer. Cut as deep as you need the mortise to be. If you're unsure, remove shallow layers until you're at the right depth. Use tape on the chisel blade as a depth guide. If you're chiseling an open-sided mortise, measure and mark the proper depth on the edge.

Chisel a uniform series of cuts along the mortise's length and, when the cuts are complete, flip the chisel over and chisel under the cuts, removing the waste to create a clean mortise.

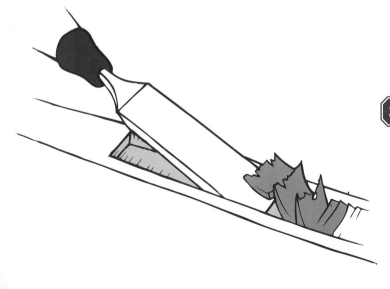

Recaulk a Tub

Create a nice surprise for her for the next time she takes a shower or a bath by cleaning up that grody mess along the seam where walls meet tub. You'll also be doing your house a favor, because a compromised caulk bead allows water to get into the wall, where even grodier mold can grow.

Before you get down to the actual caulking, you need to thoroughly clean out the existing seam so that the caulk has a stable surface to which it can adhere. (Number one reason for failed caulk seams? Unstable underlying crud that undermines the bond between the caulk, and the tub and wall surfaces.) Use a utility knife to scrape all the old caulk and other debris out, then scrub the area with rubbing alcohol to remove any remaining dirt and organic matter.

The caulking itself is easy, but it's also commonly done wrong. So pay attention. Put the tube of clear kitchen and bathroom caulk in a caulk gun and cut the tip at an angle, so that the opening is slightly smaller than the caulk bead will be. Use a smooth, consistent motion to lay a uniform bead of caulk all the way around the seam. Go slow and steady and the result will be beautiful.

Finish off the seam by using a jointing tool coated with a little olive oil or, more handily, your finger dipped in water. Run your finger along the caulk bead, smoothing it into a fluid, attractive (or at least not messy) line. Keep dipping your finger in water as you work and use a light, even pressure. This way you avoid pulling up big clumps of caulk.

Do it right, and the seam will be almost invisible, and her appreciation for a nice clean place to bathe is sure to be anything but.

Split Wood

Splitting firewood is actually more about technique than brawn. Wear eye protection, gloves, and work boots, and set the log on end on a flat, level surface. Use a splitting maul rather than an axe. Avoid hard surfaces such as driveways because the maul can go all the way through and strike the concrete.

Raise the maul with your dominant hand near the head and the other held low on the handle. Stand with your feet shoulder width apart, and bring the maul down near the edge. As you bring it down, create a whipping motion with your hips and slide the top hand down to meet the bottom hand.

Look at the strike point for the entire downward stroke. Repeat until you've split off a piece of log. Reposition as necessary to make subsequent splits.

Sharpen a Mower Blade

Tearing rather than cutting grass blades leaves your lawn primed for disease. That's why every man needs to keep his mower blade sharp.

Sharpen it at the start of, and at least once during, the season. Prop the mower on its side, exposing the underdeck. Jam a wood scrap between blade and deck to securely hold the blade. Loosen the mounting bolt and remove the blade.

Clean it, check for damage that would indicate replacement, and lock it in a vise. With the blade horizontal, file the cutting edge with a mill file at 45 degrees. File the opposite side the same number of strokes and, when sharp, remove and balance it. Slide the blade's mounting hole over a nail sticking out of a wall stud. The blade should hang level. If it doesn't, file the heavier side and keep rechecking the balance until it's right.

Fix a Fluorescent Shop Light

Your workroom is your sanctuary. Glass jars full of various nails, screws and odds and ends, with their lids nailed to the rafters? Check. Boom box left over from the '70s? Check. Trestle worktable? Check. Buzzing overhead? Wait a minute. That's not right. It's time to fix that fluorescent light to return your sanctuary to the way it should be.

Unplug the fixture, take it down and set it on a level work surface. Remove the bulb by carefully twisting it out of its mounts on either end. If the bulb has been flickering in addition to the buzzing, you may want to replace the bulb before it totally fries the ballast.

The ballast is your next point of concern. If you've just been dealing with a loud buzzing, it's probably the ballast. Pull the cover off (usually right behind where the bulb, or bulbs, sit) and you should see a small rectangular piece—one for each bulb. Remove the ballast and take it with you on your trip to the hardware store. Once there, you're going to discover a disconcerting truth—depending on your fixture, replacing the ballast may approach the cost of a new fixture. So it's your call. But if you love the fixture and it's exactly perfect for the space to kick in the loot for the new ballast.

The wiring of the ballast may seem a little intimidating at first, but chill. Ballasts come printed with a wiring diagram on their bodies. Just go slow and steady, wire by wire, and you'll hook it up in no time. Plug in the fixture, check that the new ballast doesn't have its own buzzing problem. Then put everything back together the way you found it, remount the fixture, and get back to your puttering.

Sockets

Ballast

Starter

Sockets

39

Use a Paint Sprayer

With the proper preparation, a paint sprayer can make a large indoor or outdoor painting project a cinch to complete in a fraction of the time you'd take using a roller and brush. Of course, do it wrong, and spray painting can mean covering every surface from wood floors to prize foundation plantings to the family dog in the same color as the surface you're painting. Not so good.

To do the best job possible, you'll need a spray gun you can trust. For large jobs, that means renting a compressed air or electric gun. Either one will be equipped with a filter meant for use with either latex or oil-based paint. Make sure you have the right filter or there will be tears. And some guns require that the paint be thinned. Check with your rental professional or the manufacturer's instructions; use the wrong paint or the right paint incorrectly and you can void a warranty or a rental agreement. Pay close attention to the instructions or you could wind up owning a gun that shoots blanks.

If you're using your own gun, use a paint sieve to filter the paint before you load the canister. You can find sieves at paint stores and home centers, or make your own by securing a piece of cheesecloth across the top of a pail. The last step before you get spraying is to mask off those areas—such as windows and floors—you don't want painted. Make sure you use plastic or other non-absorbent material, taped completely down over the surface. One little unsecured seam or rip can mean a lovely spatter pattern across glass or hardwood.

Test the sprayer and hone your technique on a scrap piece of plywood or cardboard, adjusting the spray nozzle to achieve the appropriate spray pattern. Once you're satisfied your gun is good to go, gear up with a respirator and safety glasses (and the more clothes coverage you have, the better for ease of cleanup).

The day you choose to paint should be calm, not windy (unless you're spraying inside). When spraying across the surface, move your hand, not the spray nozzle. Pivot your wrist as you move along to keep the spray directly perpendicular to the wall. At the end of the surface, let go of the trigger but continue your motion to ensure a smooth finish. Never run the gun dry because you can burn out the motor. Check the paint canister often to prevent this.

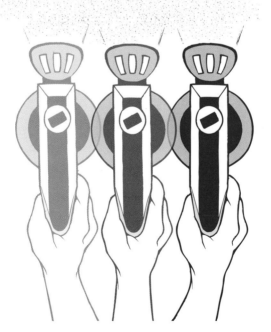

CHAPTER № 2

Wild Ways

YOU ARE NOT FOOLED BY A HANDFUL OF DISCOVERY

Channel programs. You know that venturing out into the wild is the primal test of a real man. Ruling the great outdoors takes a lot more than a few Boy Scout merit badges and a compass. You know that you have to be dialed in like a ninja, because like the ninja, you will be forced to use anything you can find in your environment to your advantage. And one hopes this book is within easy reach in your environment, because this particular chapter covers the full gamut of Jeremiah Johnson skills, from basics like starting a fire, to the real down-and-dirty, like fighting sharks mano-a-fin.

That's right, warrior. There's simply no room for smelling the posies in the great outdoors; a real man understands it's a sheer struggle for survival. You don't need to know how to identify wildflowers. You need to know how to make shelter, find nutritious and life-preserving food, keep yourself out of danger from larger or more powerful predators, and remain sane and in one piece until you return to civilization. With the right collection of knowledge and skills, you'll show the wild who's boss alright. Boo yah.

No man is born knowing how to master the great untamed world beyond civilization's borders. We don't have a manskill gene that helps us inherently know how to start a fire, or find water where it seems there is none. We aren't adapted to living among the trees and rocks, just like a wolverine would have a hard time figuring out how to pop a beer. Surviving in wolverine land as a man means acquiring the skills you need, learning the ways of the wild.

That's why we've include a full range of wilderness skills in this chapter. It might be that you only need a comfy, cozy place to bed down for the night without worrying about mama bear and her hungry husband. Or perhaps you're jonesing for a little protein to maintain your muscle mass. Maybe you've gotten a little off the beaten track and need to figure out a new road back to where your car is parked. Well, look no further. The answers you need are thick in the pages that follow, because knowing everything you need to know out there can mean the difference between getting home safely and truly becoming one with the environment.

Build a Debris Hut

A debris hut is the most basic of shelters for times when there are no rentals available on the market because there's no market on the market. Keeping warm and dry isn't just a matter of base survival, it also improves your mental state for the other challenges you'll need to answer out there in the scary black yonder. When you're deep in the woods or anywhere in the wild, this structure can offer enough protection to keep you warm and dry until you figure out your next move.

As with all things real estate, the secret to a comfortable debris hut is location, location, location. You want to find a place that is not too exposed to the wind, sun, or rain, but is also not so deep in brush or dense forest that it's hard to move around in and susceptible to visits by members of the local Wolves and Pumas Association.

Find a strong, relatively straight branch, preferably at least 5 or 6 feet long and at least 3 inches in diameter. This will be your ridgepole—the spine of your debris hut. The ridgepole can be positioned horizontally between two trees, or on a downward slope between a tree and a rock formation or the ground. The ridgepole should be at least 3 feet off the ground at the high end (the higher it is, the more headroom you'll have, but the more work it will take to complete the shelter). Either way, each end of the pole should be wedged securely in a rock crevice or the crotch of a tree. If you can't find two supports, you can wedge one end of the ridgepole in a tree crotch, and secure the other into the ground, held fast with large rocks.

With the ridgepole in place, search for the walls of your structure. Large boughs from evergreen trees make excellent walls. You can even break them right off the tree in an emergency (survival tends to trump environmentalism). Use other large branches to create a supporting

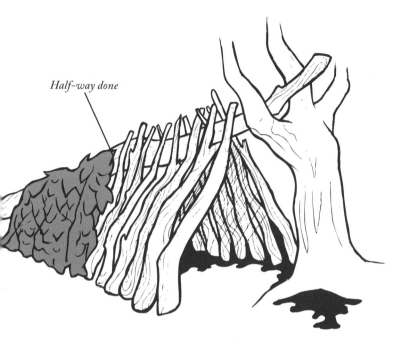

Half-way done

framework, leaning the branches against the ridgepole. Fill out this basic structure with increasingly smaller pieces, using large sections of brush and dead bushes, oversized twigs and even leaf litter, needles and moss. The drier the material, the better. It helps to shake the material out thoroughly before placing it on your shelter, to prevent sharing with insect roommates.

Finally, pile more large branches on top of the fill material to hold everything in place, and clear the floor of rocks and other sharp objects. The Taj Mahal it ain't, but a well-constructed debris hut can keep you relatively comfortable until help arrives or you figure out the next step in your survival plan.

Find Water

You can actually go weeks without food, but without water? Not so much. Water keeps the body functioning, maintains energy and body heat, and a keeps your mind clear. That's why hydration is key if you're going to survive for any significant amount of time in the wild. Luckily, there's plenty of water in just about any outdoor environment, if you only know where to look.

Your first line of defense is to not die of thirst while you're on the hunt for water. That would just be too ironic. Conserve your energy and moisture by staying out of the sun and not exerting yourself. If you have limited water supplies in a canteen or bottled water, keep it cool and drink sparingly.

Realize that you'll rarely find nature's spigot by just meandering around. Instead, channel your inner detective. Because water follows gravity, look for natural runoff areas such as the gulley between two hills or a shallow creek bed (even if the bed is dry, follow it and you may find small pools or puddles along its course). You'll want to keep an eye out for ideal spots, such as a level area at the base of an incline—especially if it's shaded and otherwise protected from the elements that might cause evaporation.

You should also investigate areas that look especially green, or seem to display an abundance of insect and plant life (humans aren't the only life forms that get thirsty, you know). If you have a sharp eye, you can follow small game tracks, because inevitably they'll lead to a water source. Just be quiet about it; large predators often follow the same clues in looking for their next meal, and you don't want to become a bear snack on your way to the watering hole.

Tie the Ultimate, All-Purpose Knot

Certain skills are part of the Swiss Army Knife collection; abilities useful in so many places that once learned, you wonder how you ever got along without them. Tying a bowline knot—sometimes called a bowline hitch—is one of those skills. The knot creates a loop of rope that can be used to secure a tent, make a snare, or for any of a thousand other purposes.

Hold the line in one hand and the end in another. Loop the end over the line to create a loop and leave enough rope in the end to create a 6. Put the end back through the loop of the six and continue it back under the body of the rope. Pull it back through the loop (the opposite direction you went through the first time). Tighten the knot by pulling on both sides, and the knot should cinch down on a loop.

Avoid a Bear Attack

Yeah, yeah, you're a tough guy. But when it comes to you versus a 900-pound, angry beast with razor sharp claws and teeth like Ginzu knives, you lose. So if you encounter a bear on your next camping adventure, keep your wits about you and avoid a confrontation you would be sure to regret.

As soon as you notice a bear, go silent. Make as wide a circle as possible around it. Keep your eye on him, while making yourself as small as possible by turning sideways or crouching. Move slowly and avoid the temptation to run. Use peripheral vision because anecdotal data suggests bears consider eye contact an act of aggression. Read the bear's body language to determine how much danger you're in. A bear shows aggression by swinging its head back and forth, breathing heavily and growling. However, rearing up on its back legs doesn't necessarily mean it's ready to throw down. It may just be trying to get a better look. If you're far enough away, it may not register you as prey or threat.

In most cases, you can slip away undetected; bears normally only attack when they feel threatened. But in rare cases, an extremely hungry bear will be on the hunt for any food source. You'll do in a pinch.

If the bear is tracking you, make noise and let it know you know it's there. Should he actually approach in a menacing fashion, don't run. Sadly, bears are way faster than you.

Instead, make noise and look for rocks and sticks to throw at the bear. If it actually attacks, curl into a ball protecting your neck with your hands and let nature take its course. Usually, the bear will stop once he thinks you're dead. But stay down—bears sometimes hang out to confirm the kill.

Stop a Hornet Attack

You might think bees are bad, until you come up against a squad of angry hornets, yellow jackets, or wasps. Bees sting once before they kick the bucket; their wild cousins can go all night.

Fortunately, it's pretty easy to prevent a nasty confrontation with these foul-tempered insects. Before you go out into the wild, apply a liberal coating of insect repellent containing DEET. Avoid cologne, flowery shampoos, or scented deodorant. Allergic to bee stings? There's a good chance you're one of the two million Americans who are allergic to wasp, hornet, and yellow jacket stings too. Carry the necessary medication such as an Epinephrine shot.

When you come across a nest, leave it alone and detour out of the area. Ditto for individual hornets you encounter. You may feel like swatting one, but you don't want to find out how many friends it has nearby just looking for a fight.

Sometimes though, you're just in the wrong place at the wrong time. Hornets nest overhead, but yellow jackets will make their nests in rotted stumps or the abandoned burrows of small rodents. That means you might walk right over a nest. If you find yourself swarmed, don't hesitate, and don't fight back. If there is water nearby, jump in. Otherwise, run. Although it will hurt, run through the thickest brush you can. Reeds are great, dense undergrowth is better. Pull your shirt up over your head to protect your head and neck, and keep running until the vicious little jerks give up.

Treat all those stings with ice if you have it, cool mud if you don't. Clean the sting sites and use a paste of baking soda and water to relieve pain. Any signs of allergic reaction such as trouble breathing or excessive swelling merit a trip right to the emergency room.

Build an Igloo

Whether it saves your life when the plane goes down on frozen tundra, or just helps impress the hell out of your friends when winter camping, igloos are just plain cool.

Although you can build an igloo with just an ice ax, it's best if you have an ice saw (but really any saw will do). Ski or snowboard edges are handy for shaping the blocks.

Choose a location that is level or gently sloped, with at least 3 feet of snow pack underneath. Mark out the base, but don't be too ambitious. Room for two people to lie down in fetal position is a good size.

Mine blocks from a compacted snow bank. Dig a hole about 3 feet in diameter and 3 feet deep, and cut out your blocks. The sides of the blocks should slant slightly inward to create the circle of the igloo. The tops are slanted down toward the inside to form the dome shape. You can trim to fit even once the blocks are in place.

Start with blocks as large as you can reasonably carry. The blocks of each successive layer should be smaller and, after the base layer, the blocks should be cut with a slight arc on the bottom. The final block that seals the top should be shaped like the lid on a Halloween pumpkin.

Cut the entrance after you finish. It should be on the slope's downside, dug below the igloo's floor, and should be just large enough for you to get through. This allows heavier cool air to flow out, while trapping warmer air inside. Cut a small vent hole to release carbon dioxide. Pour cold water over the finished structure to reinforce it. Pack snow all around for extra insulation. Light a candle or Sterno for warmth, and chill out.

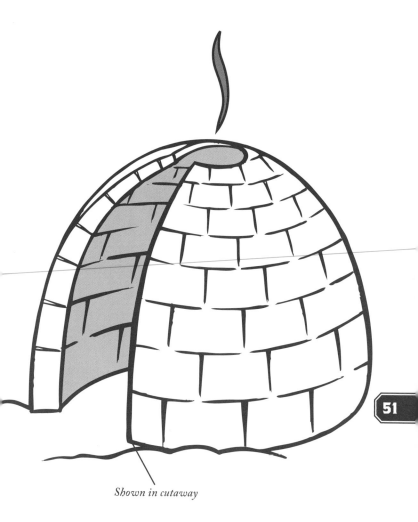

Shown in cutaway

Stitch Your Own Wound

It's just your luck to take a nasty tumble on a three-day camping trip. Open up a deep 6-inch gash on your leg and, now what? Ideally, you'll hustle to an emergency room for some tailoring. But if that isn't an option, it's time to channel your inner Jason Bourne and sew that thing up all by yourself.

Before you do anything else, stop the bleeding. Apply firm constant pressure on the wound with the cleanest cloth you can find. Even if it hurts, keep the pressure steady because losing too much blood is the most serious danger you face right at the moment.

Once the bleeding has stopped, you need to clean the wound to prevent infection. Run water over it for at least three minutes and then use whatever else you have in the way of disinfectant—hydrogen peroxide, iodine, even clear alcohol such as gin or vodka. Remove any grit, dirt or foreign bodies in the wound, as long as it doesn't entail digging it out and starting the bleeding all over again.

Now find a needle. It can be small or large. As a last resort, you can even straighten out a small fishhook. Collect the cleanest thread or fishing line you can lay your hands on, the thinner and stronger the better. Tie the thread securely to the end of the needle.

Grit your teeth and remember, pain is all in your head. Start suturing at one end of the wound, making your entry and exit puncture points as far from the wound's edges as the wound is deep (to ensure proper holding power). Skin is tougher material than you might imagine, and a doctor would use a clamp to pull the needle through the skin—you can use the pliers on your all-purpose tool if you have it with you, or just use your fingers if you don't. The sutures will be tied off with a basic square knot, in which you loop both ends through each twice (it's like two intertwining U's of thread). Pull the knot down tight, but not so tight that you cut off

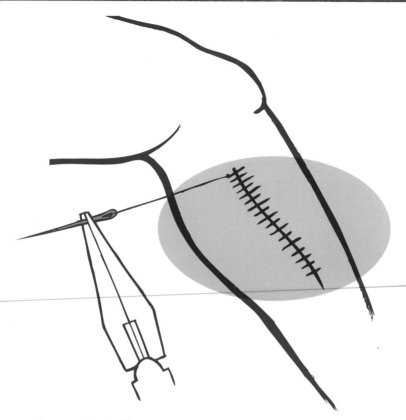

circulation to the skin. You just want to close the wound securely.
Position the knot so that it is off the line of the wound where it could
cause pain, and clip off the thread. Continue with individual stitches
in the same manner until the wound is closed.

Once the suturing is out of the way, the biggest risk is infection. Keep the
wound covered with a sterile (or as near to sterile as possible) dressing and
seek medical help as soon as possible. After all, even Jason Bourne gets
checked out once in a while.

Purify Water

There's only one thing wrong with that burbling stream you've come across in your hike: as delicious as that water looks, you have no idea what type of animal might have died on the bank upstream, or is using the stream as a latrine.

Bad water can lead to cramps, diarrhea, and vomiting that can make the trip back to civilization a tiny piece of hell, so take precautions to ensure your drinking water is safe to, well, drink. At a stream, you're already ahead of the game. Moving water is less likely to harbor dangerous bacteria than standing water. Draw water into a container with a shirt secured over the container's mouth to filter larger particles. There are several ways to protect against those smaller microbials. If you've thought ahead, you'll be carrying iodine or chlorine tablets (chlorine kills both bacteria and viruses, while iodine only works on bacteria).

In the absence of purifying pills, boil the water. Bring it to a full boil over a campfire for 5 to 10 minutes. No vessel to boil water in? Filter the water through a clean sock filled with alternating layers of sand and chunks of burned wood.

If you're stranded with no body of water in sight, dig a hole and place a container in the center. Stretch plastic such as a tarp (in the extreme circumstance, substitute a window from the crashed plane) over the hole, propping it up with rocks. Punch a hole in the center of the plastic right over the center of the container, and place a light rock or stick next to the hole to create a slope from the outer edges to the center. It's going to take a long time to get a small amount of water, but in a pinch, it's better than dying of thirst.

Get Found Before You Die

So you've managed to get yourself so lost in a national wilderness area that you have no idea where you are, where you came from, or how you're going to get home. Should have spent a little less time watching the game of the week, and a little more time on TLC shows. You are now a walking advertisement for the buddy system and a reliable GPS.

But hindsight is always 20-20. Put your regrets aside and focus on the fundamental notion of getting found. Basically, when you are so lost that you have absolutely no faith in your ability to get yourself to civilization, start with the basics. That means WFS: Water, food and shelter, in that order. You need to keep yourself in one place and keep your body going until rescuers find you. Stay near any source of water you can find, build a debris hut or lean-to and a fire, and hunt locally for anything resembling food.

Be very economical in your actions. You want to conserve energy and calories even if it means doing nothing and being bored. Keep your fire going as big as circumstances allow, but be as quiet as possible unless you know rescuers are in the area. You want to attract the notice of other people, not hungry wolves looking for takeout.

In some cases, your campsite simply won't accommodate a long stay, or weather may be so inclement as to threaten your well-being. If you have to move on, find a river or stream and follow it in the direction of the flow. Chances are that the course of the river will eventually come to some structure or campground situated on its banks. As long as there isn't some toothless guy with a banjo sitting there, you should be okay.

Navigate Without a Compass

You're so lost that even you, real man that you are, would ask directions. If only there was anybody out there to ask. Take heart, intrepid hiker. There are plenty of ways to establish the basic directions and find your path out of the wild. All it takes is an old-style analog wristwatch. Take the watch off and, holding it horizontally, turn the watch so that the hour hand is pointing to the sun. Divide the space between the hour hand and twelve o'clock, and run an imaginary line through that spot: that's your north-south line. Figure out the actual compass directions by the position of the sun—after noon it's in the west, before noon, it's in the east.

No watch? No sweat. Mark the tip of a shadow cast by a stick or tree, using a rock as marker. Wait an hour and mark the tip of the shadow again. Draw a straight line between the two marks, and that's east to west (sun rises in the east, sets in the west).

But maybe you don't know from directions. Maybe the best you can do is tell that you came from somewhere "over there." Don't just start walking because humans, left to their own devices, will inevitably walk in circles for reasons too numerous to discuss.

Establish a sight marker in the direction you want to head. Find two objects in that direction, one near, and one far. Line them up visually. Now start hiking and keep those objects lined up. When you reach the near point, do it all over again with a new far visual reference point, married to the now-near reference point. Using this method, you'll never waste time going in circles, and you'll eventually find your way back to the land of the GPS.

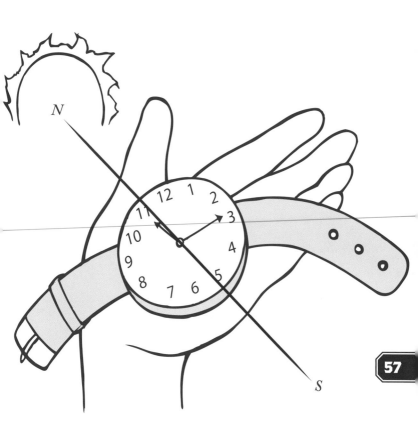

Start a Fire

Fire is one of those things separating us great naked apes from the rest of the animal kingdom. A little ingenuity is all you need to make your own. First, gather a base of tinder—anything small and combustible, such as leaves, twigs or even dried out pine needles. Gather foot-long sticks the thickness of Harry Potter's wand, and a pile of thicker logs, 2 to 3 inches in diameter. All these should be as dry as possible. If it's cool to the touch, it's too wet to effectively ignite.

Mound the tinder in a cleared area of dirt bordered with stones. Create a cone of the small sticks over the mound. Light the tinder and let the cone of sticks catch fire before layering the thicker wood logs on top of the cone.

Of course, the trick is starting the fire without your trusty Zippo. Don't bother trying to rub sticks together. Instead, find a reasonably flat piece of wood like a thick peel of bark, a straight stick as thick as your finger, and a wadded-up piece of clothing like a shirt. Create a bow by tying a shoestring at either end of another long stick. Notch out a small V in the bark. Jam the most pointed end of the stick into the notch and cluster tinder around the base. Slide your improvised bow over the stick. Hold the top of the stick with the wadded-up shirt, and begin moving the bow back and forth to spin the stick until it sparks the tinder.

You can also use the magnification method. Focus the sun's rays on tinder with the lens from a camera, glasses, or a clear, water-filled bottle. Be watchful with your fire so that it doesn't spread, and always completely extinguish it before moving on.

Stop a Shark from Eating You

Humans generally aren't on a shark's menu. But when you're in the wrong part of the ocean at the wrong time, they'll make an exception. Fending off a taste-testing shark is different than fighting off other predators: you never play dead with a shark.

A shark in the vicinity is not necessarily a sign of an imminent attack. However, if it bumps you and glides away or circles, you're about to do battle. Undoubtedly you'll feel a little uncomfortable because you're a land animal who's not on land. But taking on a shark means putting on your best alpha-dog face and going for blood.

Always keep him in front of you. If you're with another swimmer, position yourselves back to back. Sharks are crafty and they prefer to strike with surprise on their side. Be ready for them and you chalk up points in the potential survival column.

Look for any weapon. A spear gun is great, a knife is good, and a rock or broken piece of coral will serve. Cause enough pain and damage and the shark will go looking for easier prey. Injured sharks often go from predator to prey, and they know that.

When it comes at you don't flail. Pick your shots, aiming at the eyes and gills. Although sharks carry a wealth of sensors in their snouts, it's a common misconception that hitting them there will repel them. It won't. Focus on attacking. A shark is too fast to evade, so if you center your attention on keeping out of his teeth, you'll lose the battle. Damage the eyes and gills even if you get injured and you leave yourself a fighting chance at making it. Once you've repelled the killer, get to the boat or land and seek out help for your inevitable injuries.

Clean a Fish

Maybe you thought your job was all done when you popped that trout out of the water. But your mama's not part of the camping crew, so you're just going to have to step up and clean and gut that thing all by yourself. Start by cleaning the fish with fresh water to get all the slime and dirt off it. Then scale it with the back of your knife, or a fish scaler if you have one. This isn't necessary if you're just going to skin it, and some types of fish are smooth-sided and don't need to be scaled. But keep in mind before removing the skin that it's responsible for keeping most of the moisture in the fish and will keep the fish succulent when you cook it. And you love succulent, don't you, bucko?

Set the fish down on a flat, stable, level surface. You'll be using a sharp knife, so you don't want things shifting as you work. A tree stump or picnic table will serve the purpose. Use a sharp knife to slice the fish in one smooth cut from the base of the tail all the way to the head. As usual, always slice away from your body (or anyone else's, for that matter). Pull all the guts out and discard. Get every last bit in there, buddy. After you're done, rinse the cavity well with fresh water. A fast-running stream is great for this. Cut off the head (unless a fish staring at you while you eat it doesn't skeeve you), and remove the dorsal fin and gills. Cut along the side of the fin and pull it out with pliers. Wash the fish one last time thoroughly and keep it on ice until suppertime. Look at you, wouldn't Mama be proud.

Shoot a Handgun Like Wild Bill

Just packing a pistol doesn't make you a good marksman. Practice and good technique do. It comes down to stance, grip, sighting, and trigger pull, four basics that can be frustratingly difficult to master.

Like most physical skills, shooting a handgun accurately requires a solid base. A good marksman's stance creates a solid triangle. Your legs should be shoulder width apart, with the leg corresponding to the trigger hand posted back as you would if you were sliding a refrigerator into place. The opposite leg should be forward with the knee slightly bent. This base resists the gun's recoil, and gives you a stable platform for aiming. Hold the shooting arm firm but not rigid, elbow bent slightly to absorb recoil. The gun itself should be held slightly higher than your shoulder. or your line of sight will be off.

Handguns are engineered to be held in a certain way for accuracy. Your hand should be high up on the handle, thumb extended down across the grip. Hold the gun as firmly as possible without shaking.

When your stance is set and you've got a good grip, aim. You can't look at the target, front and back sights all at once. Sight the target and point the gun. Then focus on the front sight right through pulling the trigger. This will give you the tightest grouping of shots.

Finally, pull the trigger using firm, even pressure. The actual moment of the shot should be a surprise, but the fact of the shot should not. Don't jerk or you'll pull the gun off the target. Don't get frustrated if your shots go wide. It takes thousands of repetitions to make the process second nature. That's why they invented shooting ranges: because expert marksmanship is like getting to Carnegie Hall. Both take practice, practice, practice.

Snare Small Game

Caught out in the wilderness, it should be fairly easy to find water if you use your powers of observation. Shelter of one kind or another can be built with minimal effort.

And that leaves food. Sampling berries or plant life is problematic unless you happen to know which are poisonous and which are not. Besides, it's hard to take in enough calories on rabbit food alone. What you need is the rabbit.

That means snaring or trapping an animal. The first trick is to find the animal. Look closely for trails or paths. Trails are made by a variety of animals and probably won't lead you to the small game you want. Instead, find less distinct paths of broken vegetation that evidence a smaller animal. Track the animal back to its den or warren.

There are many kinds of snares and traps, ranging from the rudimentary to the amazingly complex. Working from the assumption that you're hungry and don't have an engineering degree, stick with the simpler basic snare. Tie cord—or better, wire—to a stake, and loop the other end with a basic bowline knot (page 47) so that it will close over your dinner's neck. Now suspend it right over the opening, using twigs and vines to keep the loop open, in place and hidden.

Make sure you don't leave a scent that would put your prey on alert. The easiest way to mask your humanity is to cover your hands with the slimiest mud you can find. Keep leaves between your fingers and the wire when tying the noose and setting the snare in place. Once everything's a go, sit back and wait. Or, if you're really motivated, find more warrens and set more snares. Because in the wild, you never know where your next dinner might come from.

Catch a Fish without a Rod and Reel

Figures that you're most likely to come across a trout-crowded stream the one time that you're not packing your pole. That means you'll have to be a bit more creative snagging those fish. When the fish are running close quarters in shallow clear water, try spear fishing. Find a fairly straight branch 3 or 4 feet long and cut the tip into a point. Or search for a branch with a thicker end and whittle the tip into several different points.

Take a lazier tack by setting lines over the water. Thorns or even sturdy twigs can be shaped with a knife to make excellent hooks. Braid young vines together, or use your shoelaces, for lines. Hang the set lines from a line or branch run between two trees or rock outcroppings over a stream. Bait the lines with worms or small insects, weight them with pebbles, and wait for a delicious meal to snag itself.

Make a Meal out of Insects

Extreme hunger can certainly clear up some misunderstandings. You may have thought of insects as mere pests in your lawn or annoyances at your backyard cookout. But lost in the wild, with no tracking skill to help you find small game, bugs can provide a nutritious meal when you need it most.

There's a lot to recommend creepy crawlies as a food source. They're easy to find and easy to catch. And pound-per-pound, insects can be a better source of protein than red meat.

Of course, all that doesn't make them any easier to stomach. So it's a good thing you're a real man, right? Look for a good food supply under rocks, or in moist shaded areas with rich loam. Turn over a few square feet of soil and you're sure to find some snacks to start with.

Soft-bodied insects are going to be the easiest to catch, prepare, and eat. Grubs and larvae are prolific and can be found throughout the wild with just a modicum of digging. Hard-bodied insects are tougher on your digestive system and are more likely to contain toxins. However, cicadas, crickets, ants, and other common hard-bodied insects are great food sources.

Most insects you'll come across are edible, although you may want to keep away from spiders and other stinging and biting critters for practical reasons. And be aware that red and orange are nature's warning colors. Better to stick to a diet of bland-colored food.

You can eat your insects raw, but boiling them has the added benefit of neutralizing some toxins. Cook them alive to retain their nutritional value. Pan-frying is another good way to prepare insects. A little oil and wild garlic helps most any creepy meal go down easier. Whether it comes back up is another matter.

Shoot a Bow and Arrow

Thinking of hunting Robin Hood style? You better have your accuracy down if you're going to bring home the big game. Shooting an arrow through the red dot is probably a little harder than you remember from your Camp Winnemucca days.

Assuming your hardware is up to snuff (your arrows should be a couple inches longer than the distance from your chest to fingertips with your arm extended straight out in front of you; bow size is relative to arrow size), you'll need the perfect technique to hit a target at a distance.

Stand as if the imaginary centerline running straight back from the bull's-eye were a wall in front of you. Your legs should be spread just slightly more than shoulder width apart, so that you're standing comfortably. Nock the end of the arrow right below the nocking mark on the string, holding the string with one finger above and two below the arrow, and your pinkie hanging free. Hold the bow with the other hand, tilted out at a 45-degree angle, so that the tip of your thumb is pointing at the target.

Draw the arrow back by scrunching your shoulder blades together rather than pulling with your arms. You want to use roughly equal pressure pushing the bow out and pulling the arrow back to maintain your balance and ensure a true shot. Your index finger should be right under your chin. Aim with your strong eye (the one you're most comfortable using). Sight down the arrow, aligning it with the center of the target. When you're ready, release the fingers holding the string, keeping the rest of your body absolutely still. With a little practice, you'll be bringing down that elk before he ever figures out what hit him.

Set Up a Home Survival Kit

You shouldn't wait until your own personal Katrina hits to think about an emergency survival kit. A kit only does you good if you have it at the ready. And as a former Boy Scout, you know the benefit of being prepared.

Food and water are the most important parts of your emergency kit. Freeze-dried packets of food—like those you'll find for camping and hiking—are the most efficient because they weigh little, are easy to store, and pack a wallop of nutrients. If you have the space, you can also put up canned goods. Beans and vegetables are best, but you can include prepared meals such as chili or pasta for variety. Dried pastas and beans are also smart choices for emergency food rations because they last just about forever. You'll want to lay enough provisions for about two weeks worth of eating.

You can store gallons of water but that becomes cumbersome. Instead, buy a portable water filter. Chances are that in an emergency there will be water, it just won't be drinkable. Between filtering and boiling, you should be able to make do.

Next, you'll want some basic supplies for comfort. Your kit should include a strong flashlight and extra batteries, and candles and matches. Sterno will ensure that you can cook regardless of the circumstances.

You'll also need basic first aid supplies. These should include bandages, sterile gauze, antibiotic ointment, ibuprofen or aspirin, thermometer, needles and suture thread, splint material, and backups of any prescription meds you take on an ongoing basis.

In an emergency, it's helpful to know what's going on. Keep a battery-operated or hand-cranked am-fm radio on hand. Add basic necessities such as toilet paper and a thermal blanket, and you should be suitably prepared for just about any crisis that might strike.

Outwit Pickpockets

If you think picking pockets went out with Oliver Twist, think again. The practice is alive and well in major metropolitan areas in this country and abroad.

Keep yourself from being a victim by staying aware of your surroundings. Pickpockets rely on misdirection, using common schemes like the team "bump and pick." One person bumps into you forcefully, apologizing profusely and distracting you as the partner relieves you of your wallet.

Similar scams include spilling a drink or dropping food on your jacket and then pretending to help clean if off while the real cleaning is taking place in your pocket. Experienced pickpockets can move through a restaurant, emptying jacket pockets even as the diners are sitting there, and they won't hesitate to lift a wallet from a jacket draped over your arm as you look at goods on display in a shop.

Regardless of the scam, all pickpockets look for the ideal mark. Your first line of defense is to not look like a potential mark, which means projecting confidence and awareness. In a crowded venue, scan the crowd. Someone making a beeline for you is either a friend or a potential pickpocket. If you're a visitor to the city, dress modestly. Thieves are predictably attracted to well-heeled marks.

Take other steps as well. Leave passports and valuables at home or in your hotel room. Take only the cash you think you'll need and keep it in a front pants pocket. Don't keep a wallet or cash in a jacket. If you have to carry a significant amount of currency with you, consider using a concealed money belt (even if it makes you feel like a fool; you'll feel like more of a fool explaining to the cops how someone you can't describe made off with all your cabbage).

Outlast an Undertow

Undertows are the dangerous, mysterious strangers of the ocean. When you first meet one you're likely to mistake it for just another innocent stretch of water. But then, only when it has you in its panic-inducing grasp, do you realize there is something very, very wrong.

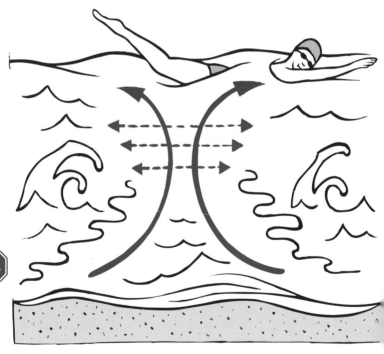

But there's no need to let an undertow make you a statistic. Surviving the experience begins with understanding what an undertow is. Technically, it's not even an undertow.

The correct term is "rip current" because it pulls you out, not under (you go under on your own). Whatever you call it, it occurs when wave action along a beach is interrupted by some sort of significant crack or dip in the underlying sand bar or shoreline. The variation causes the wave action to move back out rather than continuing along the beach, creating a robust current strong enough to pull a person back out with it.

The current itself doesn't kill swimmers. A person caught in a rip current becomes disoriented, panics, burns up his oxygen stores, and fatigues as he fights to swim back in against the current. The current usually wins that battle and, without help, the swimmer can tire to the point of slipping under the water in very little time.

The secret every lifeguard knows is that the current is actually limited in width—rarely more than 100 feet. The trick is not to fight the current, but to get out of it. That means swimming sideways, parallel to the shore. This may be a little scary because until you swim totally out of the current, you'll continue to be pulled away from the beach. But just continue swimming strongly to the side. Once you stop feeling the pull of the rip current, turn, and swim to shore.

Pick a Lock

You don't have to be a secret agent to pick a lock; most keyed locks are fairly simple devices, working on a basic pin-and-tumbler system. A cylinder turns in a housing and is kept in place—locked—when pins (actually, pairs of top-and-bottom pins) drop into the cylinder. The key pushes the top pins out of the cylinder and into the housing, allowing the cylinder to be turned and the lock opened. Picking the lock is a matter of pushing those pins up while exerting pressure on the cylinder so that the pins stay in the housing as you work on other pins.

You'll need a torsion wrench and a pick. Buy a lock-picking kit or fashion your own. Start with the wrench; it's shaped like an L and needs to be sturdy. Slide it into the bottom-most portion of the lock. Torque the cylinder open with the wrench as you work. If you're not sure which way is the open position (should be fairly obvious, and most padlocks can be opened in either direction) twist the lock in both directions. The open position should have more give than the closed position.

Use the wrench to exert force with one hand, and use the other to slide the pick into the top portion of the lock and feel your way to the individual pin positions. Start with the most resistant pin (although in some locks, they may all be the same). When you find it, push it up while turning the cylinder with the wrench. The cylinder should move a little and prevent the pin from falling back down into the cylinder. Do the same for each of the rest of the pins, always maintaining your torque on the wrench. Once you've pushed up all the pins, the lock will turn and open.

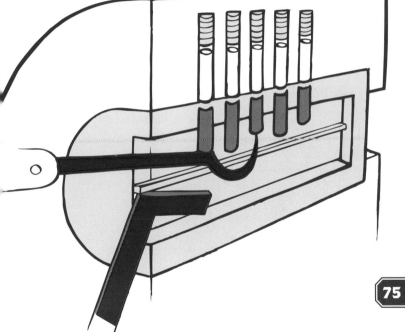

How to Fight a Dog

Fighting a dog is different than defending against a dog attack. Defense is how you get mauled. Fighting is how you teach a bad dog to behave.

Depending on the circumstance (out in the open with no weapons immediately available) you may have to resign yourself to taking some damage. Keep your wits about you and limit that to stitches rather than a blood transfusion.

Do a quick check for ad-hoc weapons. Mowing your lawn? That mower is your howitzer. A garbage can is effective (smash and bash, trap or block), as is the lid. A tree branch, a cement block, even a lawn gnome—anything heavy is going to be an advantage. Wait for him to run and jump, or lunge, and swing like you were hitting off a tee.

You naturally have an advantage because you're taller, but look for higher ground still, like the top of a car. If the dog gets ahold of you, he'll try to drag you down into the submissive position and go for your throat. Don't let him. Do the counterintuitive, and shove your hand down his throat as far as it'll go. Grab soft tissue in a death grip and use your free hand to gouge his eyes or rip off anything dangling from the undercarriage. If you managed to get on top or behind, put him in a no-holds barred chokehold, roll onto your back and squeeze for dear life. Dogs can't reach behind them, so this can be an amazingly effective strategy. Don't release him until he goes entirely limp.

Only when you think you've incapacitated him—or when he's actively heading in the opposite direction—should you head for shelter, call the authorities, and tend to your wounds. You may be hurt, but your opponent now knows who the top dog is.

Beat Jet Lag

You wake up not quite knowing where you are or what time it is. You turn on the TV and it's really no help. You feel like a truck ran over you, and you're not sure if you want to eat, sleep, or just die.

Welcome to jet lag. Real men don't let it slow them down.

Symptoms vary, but most everyone is going to experience some jet leg when they cross time zones—the more zones, the more severe the effect. We all have internal clocks that regulate our hormones, sleep cycles, and brain functions. Those clocks rely on light and external cues to keep the body running in a normal 24-hour cycle. Fly someplace far away and you mess with your internal timekeeping. This can cause disorientation, insomnia, fatigue, poor mental function and, in extreme cases, amnesia.

Key to beating jet lag is limiting factors that screw with your system and readjusting your internal time clock as quickly as possible. Avoid alcohol and caffeine on the flight. Eat light or not at all. And hydrate; water helps your body overcome most if not all the effects of jet lag.

Adjust to the new time zone by resetting your watch on the plane, and sleeping or staying awake according to your destination's time zone. This may involve a sleep mask and lowered window shade on what starts out as a daytime flight.

When you arrive, allow yourself a quick catnap—no more than 20 minutes— but then look to stay up until at least 10 p.m. local time. Going the other way, you may be full of energy at your normal bedtime, but stick to your ritual and use a natural sleep aid such a melatonin if you need to. But stay away from sleeping pills and that bedtime beer.

Throw a Punch

Sometimes there's simply no avoiding a throw down. But you can stop it quick with one well-placed punch. A solid shot to the nose makes the eyes tear up, blood flow, and nine times out of ten stops a fight cold.

A straight punch begins with your stance. Stand three-quarters profile to your opponent, with legs shoulder width apart and the leg that corresponds to your punching hand set back as a post. Bend your knees slightly.

Hold your hands 6 to 8 inches apart, with your punching hand just under your chin. Make a proper fist by curling your fingers tightly and bending your thumb under the face of the fist. Keep your wrist rigid, maintaining a straight plane along the forearm and over the top of the fist.

Now aim. Target the nose; if you miss, you're still likely to hit something that hurts. Keep your eyes on the target all the way through the punch. As things heat up, you should position yourself as if you were punching a spot six inches behind the guy's nose. This ensures follow through for maximum damage.

Unload the punch with a smooth, fluid corkscrew motion beginning with the punching-side foot. Pivot up on the ball of the foot as if you were grinding out a cigarette butt. Carry the motion through your hips, snapping them through on the punching side, and then thrust your punching shoulder forward.

Snap your fist forward, straight from the shoulder. Don't arc it; punch straight through the nose. Don't lock out your elbow. Instead, snap your arm back into a good defensive posture on the off chance he manages a counterpunch. When the blood spurts out the middle of his face and he starts to cry, be gracious. Nobody likes a sore winner.

CHAPTER № 3

Social Graces

POLITE SOCIETY IS A WHOLLY DIFFERENT JUNGLE.

The animals are more cunning, the dangers are much more hidden. And frankly, men are just much more naturally suited for hunting dinner for making it through a four-course black tie dinner. But if you're going to be the complete man, your manskills have to include a toolkit of basic social abilities.

It's not just a case of playing nice for nice's sake. How well you navigate those dark and churning social waters can determine if you get the girl you desire, get the job you deserve, and get the respect due you. Mastering this particular set of skills starts with your sartorial expertise (understanding how to dress, genius). Doesn't matter if it's your wife of ten years or that barista you see every morning at the coffee shop; women appreciate a guy who knows how to put himself together with style. Just ask James Bond.

But your look is just the simple part of the puzzle. The hard part is understanding how to behave. It's a matter of knowing how to drink with discipline so that a night of partying doesn't turn into an Internet viral video sensation. This means knowing how to order and drink wine, and the right and the wrong ways for downing harder cocktails.

We can all make it through the appetizer platter at Applebee's. It's only the truly skilled man who can handle himself with ease at a formal dinner or a three-star restaurant, and knows how to make himself at home at other social events as well. He is the panther that blends into the jungle.

You will soon be that man. It's just a matter of learning the code. A few rules, a couple new ways of doing things. It's worth the effort. Society is just waiting to reward the man who is willing to wear something grander than a track suit, say all the right things at all the right times, and generally be a truly social animal.

Tie a Tie

All those casual Fridays have shuffled the tie to back of the closet. But a well-knotted neckpiece is still a sign of a smartly dressed man. It's indispensable for rocking a special occasion, whether you're meeting her parents or just heading out to a really nice restaurant.

Getting the knot right is key to pulling off a super sharp tie-and-dress shirt combo. There are four basic types of knots, but a four-in-hand is the easiest and most adaptable. It can go casual or dressy, and it works well with thicker ties that would be difficult to manipulate into more complicated knots.

Flip up your shirt collar and slide the tie around your neck. Adjust the length of each end (the tip of the wider end should wind up hanging to the middle of your belt). Generally, the wider side should hang about a foot below the narrow side. If you're right-handed, the narrow side goes on your left.

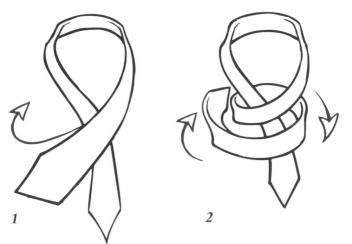

1   2

Cross the wide side over the narrow end, keeping the face out. Cross right below where the knot will be. Wrap the wide side under and around, creating a band at the top of the narrow end. Bring the point of the wide end up behind this band, loosen the band to make a loop, and pull the wide end up under your chin and down through the loop. Pull the wide end down to tighten, and slide the knot up into position on your neck. Flip down the shirt collar and check the tie. If you've done it right, there should be a dimple in the fabric right below the knot. If the length is off by more than ½ inch, undo the tie and try again. But with practice, you'll be able to tie the knot and style like George Clooney's got nothing on you.

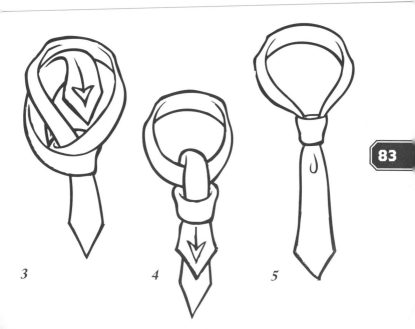

3　　　　　4　　　　　5

Iron a Dress Shirt

Few sartorial defects stand out quite like a wrinkled shirt. It's not tousled hair, or jeans with a blazer. Those things look casual on purpose. A wrinkled dress shirt simply looks like you slept in your clothes. It screams, "Hey, look at me! I'm a slob who keeps my shirts in a bag." Not really a message you want to be spreading.

On the other hand, a well-ironed shirt is one of those details that say you're a man with style and grace. It's such an easy thing to do right that there's really no excuse not to.

Set up your ironing board and iron (two more things that no self-respecting man does without), with the iron on the setting that matches the shirt fabric. Or the lowest setting if you don't know what the fabric is (which would merit a discussion on where you buy your shirts).

Iron the collar first, starting with the backside and ironing from the middle out to ensure crisp collar points. Use the end of the board as a form for the shoulder, and iron one and then the other. Then do each sleeve, one at time. Lay the sleeve flat, iron down to the cuff, flip it over, and iron the inside of the cuff. Iron the front, taking the time to get between the buttons, then the back. If you like a stiff shirt, feel free to use spray starch in the process.

Make the process a little easier by ironing your shirts right out of the dryer. It helps you see where the iron is going and gives the shirt a pressed feel, almost as if you had starched it. Hang that shirt up as soon as you're done. You want it ready to go when duty calls.

Shine Your Shoes

Shoes make the man, a small detail that separates a sharp dresser from the guy who just doesn't care. And shoes never look better than when they're sporting a fine new shine.

Use wax polish out of a can, in the color that matches the shoes. Clean the shoes thoroughly and then wrap a clean dry cloth around your finger, rub it in the polish, and rub the polish on the shoes in tight circles. Keep your free hand or a shoe tree inside the shoe to maintain the shape.

Once polished, let the shoe sit for five minutes. For a buff finish, buff the shoe with the brush or a clean cloth until the finish is uniform and attractive. If you want a high shine, buff and then spray a clean cloth with liquid window cleaner and buff over the wax until the shine sparkles. Shine your shoes every couple of weeks.

Dress for Success

Dressing for success means wearing the necessary uniform to get where you're going. If you already have millions in the bank and your own software startup, by all means, wear ripped jeans or dress like a clown for all it matters.

But if you haven't yet made the mark on the world that you hope to make, the right clothes should be part of your picture. It all comes down to dressing appropriately and not trying to reinvent the wheel.

A formal affair calls for a tux and black tie. Not a white tux. Not a powder blue tux. A classic cut black tux with black bowtie and tuxedo shirt. Cuff links mandatory. That's because a black tux is classic, and when you wear classic clothes, you say to the world that you understand that classic is, at its root, having enduring class.

The same principle applies to business attire. In business (and everywhere else) there's no such thing as being overdressed. A well-cut suit, with a tasteful dress shirt-and-tie combination are elegant in any surroundings, even one where the norm is polo shirts and khakis.

Know what dress occasions call for. A wedding means a suit and tie. An engagement party, a blazer and nice shirt, plus dress trousers. Holidays and family get-togethers, the same.

Lastly, every outfit should be finished with the right pair of shoes. Men are judged by their shoes more often than by any other piece of clothing. For dress occasions, you'll want a pair of black and a pair of brown dress shoes. Spend the money to buy quality, and both the style and the parts of the shoe will never wear out. A good pair of leather loafers are a great crossover for casual but upscale events. See? Was that so hard?

Remove a Stain

The well-turned-out manskillful man does not walk around with stains on his clothes. There's simply no excuse, because stains are so easy to defeat.

Take this rule as your mantra. Don't wipe, blot. If you spilled espresso on your shirt, rinse the spot with water and a little dish soap. If that doesn't do the trick, mix vinegar with water, blotting the stain until it disappears. Alternatively, beat an egg yolk and apply it until it saturates the fabric. Wait two minutes and flush with water.

Blood stains can be stubborn, but when caught fresh, hand washing in cold water can remove many bloodstains. As a second-level response, combine a cup of warm water, a squirt of dish soap, and capful of ammonia, and soak the stain in the mixture. Blot the stain with a damp cloth afterward to remove any traces, then rinse until the fabric is clean.

Red wine seems to find its way onto fine threads even when you're sober. Neutralize it with white wine, and then blot with a rag dampened with vinegar. Follow up by blotting with a clean, wet cloth.

Saturate a grease spot with clear-colored dish soap. Work the soap in, just enough to start breaking up the grease, but not so vigorously that you spread the stain. Blot with a clean, damp towel. It may take a few tries, but eventually you'll remove all of the grease. Then wash the clothing as soon as possible in a strong detergent.

No matter what caused the stain in the first place, make sure it's completely removed before drying any article of clothing. As soon as you dry or iron a stained fabric, you "set" the stain. The last thing you want is to ditch that new shirt just because you didn't work hard enough to ditch the stain.

Sew on a Button

Often, it's the small things that count. One missing button can draw an amazing amount of attention you don't want. And really, if you're a Manskills man, a truly self-sufficient guy, you have to know the most basic of tailoring skills—sewing on a button.

You'll find spare buttons sewn along the hem of the shirt, on the inside of dress trousers' waistband, or inside a suit coat or blazer. Invest in a small sewing kit and you'll be ready to tackle any missing fastener.

Cut a two-foot length of thread, and thread it through the needle so that the needle is halfway along the length of the thread. Tie the ends of the thread together in a knot.

Position the button where you need it. Put a spacer such as a toothpick, or a needle from your sewing kit, between the button and fabric to make sure you don't sew it too tightly. Push the threaded needle up through the fabric and through one of the holes in the button. Keep pulling the thread through until the knot prevents you from pulling any further. Now put the needle down through the opposite hole—the diagonal in a four-hole button—and back down through the fabric. Keep guiding the needle up and down through the holes, until it is securely fastened and there are an equal number of crossovers between the holes.

Now come up through the fabric once more, and circle the thread underneath the button several times around the stitches you've already made. Poke the needle back down through the fabric, and stitch through the loops of thread on the underside of the piece, creating a secure loop or knot. Cut off the extra thread, button up, and go get 'em tiger.

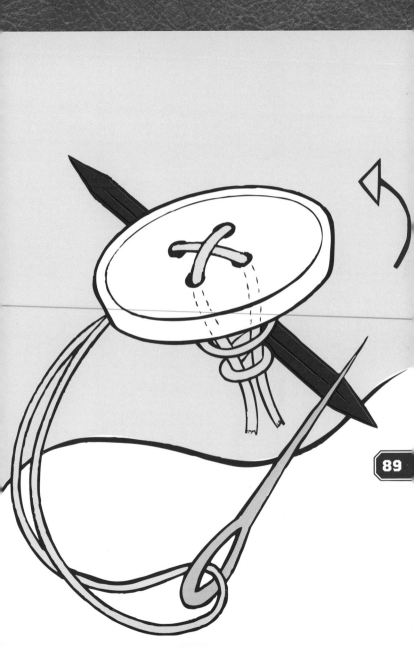

Break up a Bar Fight

It's the truly selfless man who doesn't want to see two strangers maim each other in the middle of a bar. Kudos to you if you're going to be the calmer head that prevails, but use that cool to determine if you should be getting involved at all.

Judge how serious the potential fighters are and abide by the cardinal rule: Don't get yourself mangled in the process. A quick assessment is key. Two dudes in polo shirts who've had one too many grasshoppers and are prepping for an ugly slap fight—by all means, jump in. Two giant bikers flying gang colors and snarling at each other in a drug-induced rage, not so much.

If you don't feel you can overpower at least one of the fighters, best to try words alone. In any case, words are the place to start. You can try, "C'mon, let's chill out before someone gets hurt," or a similar pearl of wisdom. Or you can go with the more effective, "Cool it, the cops are right outside."

If you actually take the plunge to break up two guys in contact, don't go it alone. Find an ally in the crowd and enlist him with "Let's stop these two fools before they hurt someone else." Never get in the middle of two combatants. The idea is to separate them out of the range of attack without putting yourself in harm's way. The best way to do that is to hook your arms under the fighter's arms. Pull him back out of fighting range with a calm, simple sentiment like, "Let it go, he's not worth it."

If all that doesn't do the trick, get yourself another beer, put ten down on the big guy with the goatee, and settle in to watch the battle.

Order Wine Like You Know What You're Doing

You don't have to be a wine snob to find your way around a wine list. You just need to know the very basics that will keep you from looking stupid. It starts with the three fundamental types of wine: red, white and rosé.

You can count out rosé. There are good rosé wines, but you're not likely to come across them. So before you're even out of the gate, you've narrowed the options down to red or white.

Assuming you really are wine illiterate, narrow the choice further with classic food matching. Meat for the main course equals red. Fish and pork equals white. Pasta in a red sauce? Red. Pasta in a white sauce? White.

With the color decided you have one more decision to make—the grape. Don't be tempted to order "red" or "white," or what you get will probably be undrinkable and your dinner companion will have pegged you as a hick long before dessert comes. What you need is an easy, all-purpose type of wine in each color. Lucky for you, they exist. Almost every wine list will carry a Cabernet (red) and a Chardonnay (white). They are the most widespread grapes in the world. So you'll always sound knowledgeable picking one or the other. But don't pat yourself on the back just yet. You still have to go through the serving ritual.

A quality wine is always tasted and approved before it can be poured. The server will open the wine, lay the cork in front of you, and pour a splash into your glass. Smell the cork (you're checking that the wine hasn't turned to vinegar), and pick the wine glass up by the stem. Swirl the sample to release the aroma, smell it and take a sip. Nod your head, and let the server pour the wine.

Tip Servers Properly

Rewarding wait help and bartenders is a mark of the experienced man about town. Just how well you reward them is a matter of sophistication, discretion, and tradition. Once upon a time, 15 percent was the benchmark. That's still good enough in a diner, but when you're out at a three-star restaurant, expect to add between 18 and 20 percent to a dinner check or bar tab.

The only reason to give less is for indisputably bad service. And even then, 10 percent should be as low as you go—it will send a strong wake-up call to the server without making you look like Scrooge.

Much as you might want to, never stiff a bartender or waiter. Not only is it considered classless (if it's about bad service, then you're stooping to their level), it's also punishing the people behind your server. Whatever tip you give likely trickles down to a busboy, a kitchen "runner," the host that sat you, and bar backs, among others. In a restaurant that "pools" tips, you'll be punishing wait help and bartenders who had nothing to do with your experience. If the service you received was aggressively abysmal, you should talk with the manager, rather than punish with a nonexistent tip.

How you tip is almost as strong a sign of refinement as how much you give. Be subtle. You don't need to make a production out of what you leave a bartender; simply walk away, leaving the money on the bar behind you. When you pay the check at your table, do it quickly and quietly, and make sure no one else at the table sees the bill. As with so many other things in the classic man's universe, discretion is the better part of valor.

Send Food Back

There's a not-so-fine line between being an overbearing pompous fool, and being someone who wants reasonable service and food in exchange for the hard-earned lettuce you'll be dropping on a nice meal at a good restaurant. Even the most gentlemanly among us has to occasionally put his foot down and demand to be treated right. And when your steak comes out ice cold and tough as a shoe, that time has come.

Keep in mind that a problem with the food is not (usually) a problem with the server, so don't take it out on him or her. Being courteous is the secret to getting what you want and making anybody else at the table feel comfortable.

When the kitchen sends out something besides what you ordered, think about whether you might just like what you got. If it's something you can eat, hush up and eat it.

But in the case of unpalatable food or something totally different than what you ordered, get the server's attention, tell her the problem, and ask her to take it back. It's always better to request a replacement (overdone meat should have been rare) than it is to request a fix (no mushrooms in the sauce) because chefs and cooks in restaurant kitchens are notoriously petulant about food being sent back. If your dish is just being repaired, you risk having something you hadn't planned on being added to the food.

Don't expect to get a reduction on the bill or any other make-good like a free dessert, because that's not how it works. If you wind up with the dish you originally ordered, prepared reasonably close to the way you ordered it, *quid pro quo* has been fulfilled.

Stop a Friend from Driving Drunk

A good man is a good friend. A good friend stops a drunk friend from getting behind the wheel. Period. The ironic part about dealing with a drunk is, the drunker he is, the less open he'll be to anything resembling reason. Given that reality, getting a drunk's keys often entails a little trick psychology or even outright flim-flammery. Whatever you have to do, don't feel bad about it; it's all for a good cause.

The easiest way is to pilfer his keys early on. If you sense where the night is going, tell your friend you left something in his car and borrow his keys. Never return them and, when he asks for them as the night winds down, play dumb, apologize, and call him a cab or give him a ride. Subterfuge is a wonderful tool in dealing with someone whose faculties are diminished.

Unfortunately, drunks can get belligerent. Chances are that once a friend is good and truly lit, he's not surrendering his keys or even entertaining rational conversation on the subject. In that situation, go at the problem from the car side. Let the air out of all four tires (a drunk can easily drive with a single flat tire, without even realizing it). An even more definitive solution—if you can get the hood up—is to disconnect the spark plug wires. If you're desperate, break off a key or piece of metal in his door lock. If he can't get in the car, he can't drive.

It all may seem like a great big hassle in the moment, but you could be saving your buddy an arrest or worse. And just think of the revenge you'll enjoy the next morning, when you wake him up at 6 a.m. with an air horn.

95

Ease a Hangover

Put down that revolver, son. It may seem like a reasonable way of dealing with the effects of last night's party fest, but there are better ways to tame a hangover. Of course, the best way is prevention. Eat a ton of food before you go out, alternate every drink with a glass of water, chug a big jar of sports drink when you get home, and sleep late.

But then again, it's not about thinking ahead, is it?

So when you roll over and feel like you need to shave your tongue, start with the basics. Hydrate. Hydrate. And hydrate. Water will be your savior. Diuretics (like alcohol) are your enemies. Which is why you should stay away from coffee and caffeinated sodas when you get up (and the hair of the dog). Even though you crave something with a kick, your body needs water and electrolytes. Lots of them.

Then take two ibuprofen for the pain. Don't be tempted into just gulping them down; along with everything else, you've trashed your stomach lining and you need to go easy on it. Lay down a foundation of salted crackers or toast. Now pound some supplements. Vitamin C (500-1000 mg), a daily B-complex tablet for men (100+ mg), and magnesium (250-500 mg) will all help. If you're up to a trip to the health food store, latch onto the amino acid cysteine (200-500 mg).

Now get some food in your system. Start slow, with a simple banana smoothie containing a little protein powder if you have it, a bit of honey, and some low-fat or skim milk. Once you're certain your stomach can handle it, transition to a vegetable drink such as V-8. If you're up to solid foods, go heavy on veggies, especially kale, cabbage, spinach, and carrots. They may not be what the taste buds are shouting for, but they are the quickest road to revitalization.

Now get moving even though you really just want to curl up and die.
A hot shower opens up your pores and allows your system to sweat out
some of the toxins. A sauna is even better. A shower alternating between
hot and cold is especially effective. A simple walk in fresh air will revitalize
you surprisingly well, although that much movement may seem a bit
beyond your capabilities, all depending on how much you indulged.

Rather than pound aspirin or ibuprofen for your headache, use a cold
cloth. And lastly, try not to think too much about what might have
happened the night before. You can
always check online for the video
when you're feeling better.

Hold a Baby

When some misguided parent shoves a newborn into your arms expecting you to show it all due adoration, manning up means putting a smile on your face and holding that little munchkin in a safe and sane way. Because babies don't come with handles, you can choose from one of two basic positions to adequately hold and protect the tiny body.

Understand first that under no circumstance are you obligated to wrap yourself in a baby sling or any other apparatus that will make you look like a fool. You're required to hold the tiny human only long enough to show you care. That can be done with your arms alone.

The "cradle hold" is the simplest way of cradling a baby, and allows you to admire the baby while you hold it (or at least pretend to admire it—some babies are, let's face, just plain ugly). Holding your arm bent and close to your body, place the baby's head inside the joint of your elbow, so that the child's body runs down your forearm. Now place your other arm draped along the outside of the baby, to ensure the infant doesn't pop out.

Too intimate? The more manly option is to use an upright carry, leaning the baby on your shoulder and bending the elbow to wrap your forearm under the baby's butt. Use your free hand to stabilize the child by bracing the neck (it will probably be too weak to hold up its own head) and the back with your fingers spread.

Now coo like an idiot and say nice things to the parents about how beautiful their baby is, and hand it off at the first chance. Hold it for thirty seconds and you've officially done your duty. Any longer and you risk diaper duty.

The man who can smoothly break the ice in a social situation is a rare gem indeed. Be that man and you'll always find yourself at the top of an invite list.

Start with confidence. Look at it this way: a minute of embarrassment isn't going to kill you. You're not risking money, health, or a job. And, in the end, most people wish they had the guts to initiate contact. Even if you fall on your face, you'll have admirers in the crowd.

But you won't fall on your face. Because you'll be prepared. As spontaneous as breaking the ice may seem, it's actually a very calculated social interaction. Approach with a purpose. Are you looking to introduce yourself to a group of women with the idea of asking a particular lucky soul to dinner? Or are you simply hoping to put people at ease and network? Know your goal, because you'll steer the ice-breaking process toward that goal—whether it's getting a phone number or exchanging business cards.

Prepare an opening line and a follow-up. "Hi" is not an opening line. Nor is introducing yourself (that's part of the follow up). People want to be engaged and entertained. Stay away from controversial subjects (politics and religion—no. The latest blockbuster movie—yes). Focus on something that might have a story behind it, like a ring, or an unusual tie. People love to talk about themselves, so play on that.

Look at it journalistically. Whatever your opening line—and you should have several generic lines in the bag—they should all end in a question. And there should be a question right behind that question. Questions lead to knowledge. Which lead to conversations. And there's the secret. Once you're in a conversation you, sir, have officially broken the ice.

Be the Best Best Man

You might look at it like a burden, but being picked as a groom's best man is one of the highest honors a friend can give another friend. So quit your whining, rent a tux, and get with the program. You've got some duties to execute.

Although the best man is responsible for the bachelor party (dude, no strippers—be a class act and throw together a poker-and-drinking party), and for holding the ring (one thing in the whole ceremony, don't screw it up), the biggest responsibility is giving the toast. Weddings are the stuff of legends and memories, so take this responsibility seriously because you really don't want to wind up on YouTube's stupid toasts of all time list.

Follow the classic toast rules: Stand up (straight, to command attention); Speak up (clearly to be understood); Shut up (quickly so that the toast is memorable, not boring).

Be witty if you're naturally witty (as expressed by other people, not that guy in the mirror). If you really have something funny and appropriate to offer, great. But be careful. Resist the temptation to recall tawdry stories of misspent youth involving antibiotics or bail (it sometimes helps in crafting your speech to imagine the bride's father as an audience of one). Otherwise, focus on speaking from your heart about your own knowledge and experience with the lucky couple. Write down your remarks to organize your thoughts and practice the toast, but when it comes time to raise a glass, don't read from a card. Be as natural as possible and to avoid nerves, look at your audience's foreheads, rather than into their eyes. Try to seem as spontaneous as possible and keep your remarks brief—the night is supposed to be about those two people represented on the top of the cake.

Dance Like Fred Astaire

It doesn't matter if you were born with two left feet; a few simple dance steps will help you fool your partner no matter what the occasion. And keep in mind that just being brave enough to get out on the dance floor earns you plenty of points.

No matter what the dance, you'll always start by putting one hand on her hip and holding the other hand out for hers. She'll put her hand on your shoulder. Don't get hand placement mixed up, or you really will be off on the wrong foot.

The tricky part is that you're the Man, man, so you are expected to lead. Your hand on her hip will guide her in following you. Be firm but don't shove.

The rhythm of the music should determine your steps, but in the worst case—where you aren't even sure what the beat of the music is—you can simply move one foot to the other, then back out, shuffling slowly in simple circles.

But feigning dancing ability means at least knowing a simple two-step pattern. Move one foot off to the side, lightly pulling her with you, and bring the other foot to the first foot, hesitating in time to the music. Then repeat the motion with the other foot, moving slightly backward in addition to side to side. This is an easy step to master and it allows you to navigate your partner around the floor, so that you approximate the actual act of dancing. It works for almost all ballroom dance music.

If you recognize the faster ¾ beat of waltz and feel a little more adventurous, try a basic box step. Step left foot to the left, and bring the right foot to the left foot. Then step toward your partner with the left foot (without stepping on her feet, put your foot between hers), and bring your right foot in line with the left, but shoulder width apart. Bring your feet together smoothly, in time with the music (you should be gently guiding her in the same pattern), and then step back with your right, after a pause to the beat so that the right foot is back in starting position. Smoothly move the left foot out to the side of the right foot to begin the pattern again.

A true gentleman never acknowledges the pain when a woman steps on his toes. Suck it up and just keep moving in your pattern, leading her with gentle pressure. You can always patch up your toes when you get home, but the middle of the dance floor is for showing off your grace in more ways than one.

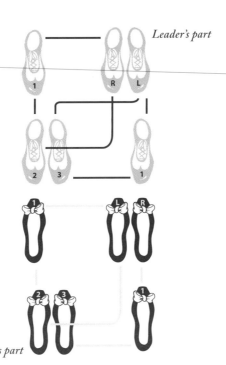

Make a Dynamite Toast

The best toasts, like the best dental work, are short and sweet. There are basically two types you'll be called upon to make: the personal tribute to someone on a special occasion, and the general toast known as a table toast. Either way, it pays to be prepared.

You can choose from hundreds of time-tested toasts that still hold water when given at the right moment. General classics such as the Irish "May the sun always be at your back and the road rise to greet you," are nice sentiments on any occasion. Or you can opt to craft a more unique toast.

If you go that route, understand that the art of the toast is saying a lot in as few words as possible. More than 30 seconds is a speech. Less than 15 seconds is a good toast; the best toasts are just one or two sentences.

You also need to follow the protocol of a toast. Timing is everything—you don't want to catch someone in the middle of a story or in the middle of unwrapping presents. Or in the middle of anything, really. Wait for a moment when the conversation is muted. Be sure everyone has a glass full of something to toast with. Then start by clinking your glass with a utensil or just stand and clear your throat.

Invite everyone to toast, but if you're toasting one person, look him in the eye as you give the toast. If you're making a general toast, look as many people in the eye as possible as you give the toast. Raise your glass (more traditional than clinking glasses, and more appropriate for large groups), and finish by taking a slug of whatever's in your glass. Then sit down and bask in the subtle glory and power of well-chosen words.

Be a Great Host

Dean Martin was the king of party hosts. Dino had a way of making people open up and have fun. Partly, he never hurt for the wry comment, but mostly it was that he seemed to be having a lot of fun himself. He knew how to put people at ease, the secret of good hosting.

Your duties actually start before anyone ever arrives. Be careful who you invite. One boor is like a bad apple—he can ruin the whole damn shindig. Invite opposites and people you think will mix well. And always bring in a few point people, adroit conversationalists that will lift any dead spots.

The cardinal rule of hosting is knowing that hungry and thirsty people make for a bad party. Provide plenty of booze and non-booze, and plenty of snacks (you know that canned cheese squirted on a Ritz does not a snack make, don't you?).

Every party also needs a soundtrack. If you want people dancing, play a dance mix and be willing to join in the gyrating. If the music is going to be background, make sure it's not so loud and thumping as to disrupt conversation, or so sleep-inducing that your guests are nodding off on the couch.

The harder part is creating the relationships that make for a memorable bash. It's your responsibility to not only introduce people, but introduce topics of interest and commonality that will kick-start conversations. Circulate around and spend just enough time in one place to get conversation rolling on safe and interesting topics like recent movies. Your guests should be able to take it from there.

Measure success by the difficulty you have in getting people to leave. If they're still there long after you want to be in your jammies, pat yourself on the back: Dino's smiling down on you.

Navigate a Formal Dinner Table

You only have to sit down for one truly formal meal to understand just how much time the upper crust of society has on their hands. Not only are they going to take forever to work through dinner, they had to set up a nearly indecipherable mix of implements for different courses.

Well, not indecipherable. There actually is a basic logic to which utensil or setting you should use when. There may be up to four utensils on either side of your plate, and they are generally placed in order of use, from outside to in. Forks go on the left. So, if you're having salad as a first course (if it's a European-style dinner, it may come last), the fork you should use is the one farthest outside. Next in will be the appetizer fork, and then the entree fork.

Same organization applies on the right. The entree knife will be closest to the plate, with the appetizer knife outside of that and, possibly, a soup spoon on the very outside.

But none of those knives are used to butter your bread, unless you're intent on showing how much of a commoner you are. A butter knife will be placed crossing the bread plate, which will be to your left (dude, do not steal any of your neighbor's stuff—that is really bad form).

A dessert spoon—or other utensil, depending on the dessert—will be placed horizontal to the table edge, at the top of the plate. You may also notice a small bowl of water with a lemon slice floating in it. Don't sip it you yokel. That's a finger bowl for cleaning your fingers. Daintily. Since you don't know how to clean your fingers daintily, wash up in the bathroom before dinner, eat carefully, and just leave the bowl alone.

The glassware may be a bit of a mystery as well. So here's the lowdown. Small stemware is for white wine. Larger stemware is for red. A tumbler is for water. Turn your wine glasses upside down if you're not drinking at the meal. Leave your water glass alone until you need a sip of water.

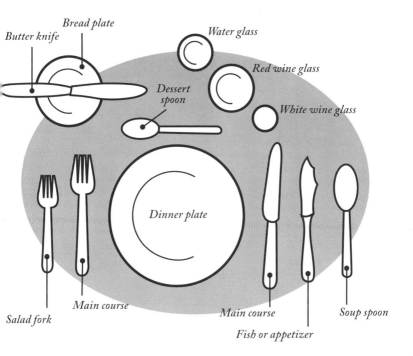

Butter knife

Bread plate

Water glass

Red wine glass

Dessert spoon

White wine glass

Salad fork

Main course

Dinner plate

Main course

Soup spoon

Fish or appetizer

When in doubt, surreptitiously watch your host or hostess. Do what they do and you'll never be found out for the bumpkin you are. Work your way through courses and don't worry if you can't figure out how to eat something or which utensils to use; it's perfectly acceptable to leave food uneaten. Much more acceptable than it is to eat at the wrong time or with the wrong instrument. And don't worry, if you leave hungry, you can always stop at White Castle on your way home.

Change a Diaper

Look, sooner or later you'll be a dad. You meet that perfect gal, you're smitten, and before you know it, down the aisle you go. A couple years later, a mini-you is on the way. So you might as well practice now, chum. And look, suffer a little poop and bottom wiping now, and be a superhero to your friends or family as a truly selfless man.

Start by getting everything together: new diaper, wipes, lotion or powder, and respirator if need be. Place the baby on a towel or large cloth, set out on a level, stable surface. Fight the urge to duct tape the little rascal down. Open the new diaper and slide it under the baby, then unlatch the old diaper. Prepare yourself. No, really. Pull the front of the old diaper down and, grabbing both the baby's ankles with one hand, lift the legs so that the undercarriage is exposed. Start wiping. Wipe like your life depended on it. It's going to take more than one wipe. Wipe from the front of the baby to the back to prevent infection. Suppress your gag reflex. Drop the used wipes in the exposed pocket of the old diaper.

Once the whole area is shiny clean, slide out the old diaper, folding it up as you go, and drop it in the garbage next to the changing table. Lower the little pooper's bottom into the new diaper, apply lotion or powder, and fold the front of the diaper in place over the nether regions. Cross the adhesive tabs to secure the diaper tightly enough to prevent leakage, but loose enough that the baby is still comfortable. You're duty is now done. Or at least until that last jar of creamed peas kicks in.

Ace That Job Interview

Rocking a job interview is about three things: preparation, preparation, and preparation. With all the info available online—not to mention in the job ad—there's no excuse for not knowing the company and job you're interviewing for inside and out.

Before you ever interview, clearly understand what place the company occupies in the competitive landscape. What are the key issues and challenges the company faces? Then pick out the three most important and relevant abilities or requirements referenced in the ad.

Create your pitch from these. Develop specific scenarios that explain how you would be a value to the company, and work on answers to all the questions you think you might be asked. Use the answers as frameworks for what you want to cover in the interview, but don't rehearse answers. Seasoned HR pros pick up on scripted replies and won't appreciate your lack of spontaneity.

Don't be afraid to be social in a job interview. You want to make it as pleasant for the interviewer as possible. Keep in mind that the over the course of the average job interview only about 30 percent of the time is spent discussing the job. The rest of that time is your chance to convince the interviewer that you'd be an interesting and positive addition to the workplace.

Be succinct. Any answer longer than 30 seconds is rambling, and you'll lose the attention and interest of the interviewer. Stories are great, but they have to illustrate a point you're trying to make, and do it quickly.

Lastly, never lie. There's too great a chance that the interviewer will do a little checking and catch you in the lie. The truth is less likely to lose you the job than a tiny lie that sours an otherwise good impression.

Conduct a Successful Business Meeting

When it comes to the world of business, perception is often reality. If everyone thinks you're the next Donald Trump, chances are forces will conspire to make you a rising star in the company. And one of the best ways to create the perception of yourself as a potential captain of the ship is to run a business meeting like a boot camp drill.

Set the stage for your meeting with an agenda. The agenda is your super tool and the whip you use to keep everyone else in line. It should clearly and simply outline who needs to be there, what they need to bring, what the goal is, the points that will be covered, and a time frame. A tight time frame. Use the agenda as your road map and execution plan.

Stand up to lead the meeting. Restate the goal at the start and again throughout the meeting. Be succinct, because rambling is a sign of corporate weakness and fuzzy thinking. When people start telling stories, arguing, or just getting off topic, don't be afraid to interrupt them and bring them back down to earth and to the goal at hand. Assign a note taker but don't do it yourself—your role is leader and delegator, and doing anything else undermines your authority. A meeting summary should be distributed the day of the meeting.

Move the meeting along briskly and give little floor or time for dissent to your decisions. End the meeting as soon as the goal is reached or the issues resolved. Short, pointed meetings are the most memorable and effective, and they speak volumes about your ability to make people get on board and do what needs to be done. Run them right, and you can start picking out the furniture for your corner office.

Ask for a Raise

You are a valuable man putting in 60-hour weeks of quality labor. A valuable man should be rewarded in recognition of his value. That's a good place to start. But it ain't going to get you a raise.

Higher pay requires a more compelling reason than, "I deserve it." Why you need the money or how you'll use it are irrelevant as well. Raises are handed out on merit. So make your case based on merit.

Prepare a list of every quantifiable achievement you've made in your current role. Focus on the exceptional or achievements outside your original job description. Be as specific as possible. Research comparable pay scales for your position throughout the industry. If you're on the low side of that number, that's another bullet in your gun. If you're at the top of the scale, you won't be mentioning comparable salaries.

Timing is everything. If your company is struggling just to keep its doors open, it's the wrong time to stick your hand out. Most companies have a cyclical and formal review-and-raise procedure. There's no law against making your case outside that procedure, but you're going to need less ammo if you ask for a raise and toot your horn during the established review process.

Whenever you take the plunge, keep it positive. Don't threaten, even if you have an offer from another company waiting in the wings. That's just asking for bad feelings, burnt bridges, and trouble. Understand that any request for a raise is usually a negotiation. Make as strong a case as possible, but if the answer is a definite "no," don't whine.

Then go back to doing the great job you've always done. If you've made a strong case, you'll eventually see more green in your pay packet.

Fire Someone Gently

The road to the top of the corporate mountain is full of potholes, but few are bigger than that moment you give someone a pink slip. Do it with grace and an eye to the details, and you'll avoid a whole lot of keening and wailing, not to mention a lawsuit.

When you make the decision to pull the trigger and get rid of deadwood, make sure your ducks are in a row. You should have a paper trail chronicling the slacker's misdeeds, and fulfilled all the pertinent points in your company's HR guidelines.

Never give the news alone. Always bring an HR rep with you, and arrange to have computer access, cell phones, and credit cards cut off while you're meeting with the soon-to-be-ex employee. Use the band-aid approach. Be quick, concise, and to the point. The person should be absolutely clear that it isn't a warning, and that there's no possibility of negotiation.

This doesn't mean you have to go all Sgt. Fury on the pour soul. Empathize. Be careful what you say, but be willing to listen and tolerate a certain amount of venting, even if it means putting up with a hissy fit and some less-than-complimentary comments. You and/or the HR representative should have the paperwork and details at your fingertips. The person should walk away knowing the exact specifics of severance, health care extensions, and potential referrals. Be thorough. You'll never regret being a little OCD about the process. You want to make it clear that the employee is leaving as soon as the meeting is over—the HR rep can clean out a desk or locker. The idea is for the termination to cause as little ruckus among the rest of your workforce as possible. And hopefully, in your day as well.

CHAPTER 4

Vehicular Savvy

TODAY'S CAR IS THE MODERN MAN'S HORSE. THERE IS A marriage of man and machine, a recognition of all the car means to a guy: independence, the thrilling possibility of travel, a chance to get away from it all and be master of your own fate. Of course, it's also a bit of an enchanted relationship. From Steve McQueen to the Dukes of Hazard, men have long been associated with their hot rides.

But like a horse, your four-wheeled machine has needs, however basic they may be. Answer those needs—change the oil regularly, rotate the tires, take care of the beast—and your car will serve you well for decades, until that fateful moment it breaks an A-arm and you have to shoot it. Or just trade it in.

Or, in the case of that '69 fastback Mustang, rebuild the thing no matter what.

Knowing how to fix what's wrong with his car is every man's protection against greedy mechanics and unscrupulous tow jockeys. It's also a way for any man to bond more fully with his favorite machine, if not just spend a Miller High Life hour in the garage with a foamy beverage, the classic rock station, and an impressive array of tools. Knowing how to drive that same car in every possible weather condition, and how to drive it for fun, is protection against personal injury and boredom.

Of course, not every man chooses four wheels. The motorcyclist taps into the cowboy's love of wide-open spaces, and the freedom and rebellion that has drawn the passion of characters from the Wild One to Easy Rider. But the two-wheeled horse presents its own handling challenges, being the most dangerous mode of transportation (part of its allure).

The complete man knows how to handle his horse no matter how many wheels it may have. That is why mastering motorized transportation is undeniably a mainstream manskill.

Jump a Dead Battery

The grand rule of car batteries: they will go and go and go, until you absolutely have to be somewhere (delivering a kidney on ice or something similar) and then fizzle. Nada. Just the lonely, heartbreaking click of the key as it tries in vain to start that engine.

Rope in a friendly passerby or use your other car if you have one, and you'll be on the road before the crucial donated organ is defrosted.

As simple as jump-starting a car is, you do have to be careful. You don't want to wind up with a permanent burn tan, or worse. An errant spark around a car battery can make it explode, but a reversed change can lay waste to the electrical systems in your car. Then how would you listen to that *Greatest Hits* of Abba tape you've been hiding from you-know-who?

Both cars should be parked nose to nose, but not touching. They should be turned off. Then follow this sequence exactly: Hook up one end of the hot—red—cable to the positive terminal of your (dead) battery. Clip the other end of the hot cable to the positive terminal on the donor battery. Clip the ground—black—cable to the negative terminal on the donor battery, and clip the other end of the black cable to your engine block or metal frame—not your battery.

Start the jump car and wait for it to idle for about 5 minutes. Crank your beast to life (or wait slightly longer if it doesn't turn over), and remove the cables in exactly the opposite order, being extra careful not to allow the ends to touch anything on either car, or each other. Finish up by thanking the good Samaritan who gave you the jump, and get that kidney where it needs to go pronto.

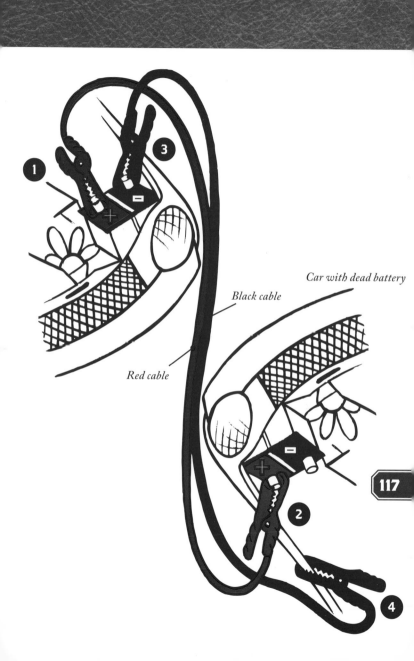

Black cable

Red cable

Car with dead battery

Change Your Oil

Yes, cars may have evolved into complex, computer-controlled monstrosities. But you're not going to surrender your automotive mastery. At least not while you can still change the oil in your ride.

This simple maintenance procedure should be done every 6,000 miles or 6 months, whichever comes first. So you'll have plenty of opportunities to regularly get in touch with your inner mechanic.

The car should be on a level surface to ensure that all the oil drains. Lay down a pad or a piece of cardboard and slide yourself under the car. Use the appropriate box wrench or ratchet to loosen the crankcase drain plug. Slide a pan under the hole, and remove the plug, making sure to keep yourself out of the stream of dirty oil. Once the crankcase has completely drained, slide the pan over underneath your oil filter and use a filter wrench to unscrew it.

Clean the threads on the drain plug and in the crankcase hole, and on the post for the filter. Screw in the drain plug just until it's snug. Don't overtighten because it's easy to strip. Now coat your finger in fresh, clean oil, and coat the gasket on the oil filter. Screw on the oil filter until it is hand tight, and then use the filter wrench to tighten it another ¾ turn.

Fill up your crankcase with the oil recommended in your car's manual—the manufacturer knows better what your engine needs than any oil company does. Remember to replace the fill cap on the engine. Wait for the oil to drain down, and check your dipstick to make sure the level is correct.

Now start your engine up and check underneath for leaks. If you see any, shut off the engine and tighten the drain plug or filter as necessary.

Get Your Car out of the Mud

Getting stuck in the mud is one of life's great frustrations. But don't be left waiting for AAA; you can get yourself out of this mess with little fuss (but lots of muss—you're in mud, remember?). Once it's clear you're stuck, stop spinning your tires.

Instead, get out and inspect the situation. It may be that if you have company, or if you're a bit of a gym rat, you can simply put the car in neutral and rock that baby out of the predicament and onto dry earth. More likely than not though, it will be too slippery to push the car free.

In that case, provide traction for the drive wheels. You'll do that by jamming something underneath the drive tires. Boards will work. Big pieces of thick cardboard—like the walls from a box used to ship refrigerators—are also pretty effective. Barring anything else, you can use your floor mats, but be prepared to get them filthy. If you don't even have floormats (dude, what are you driving, a '74 Gremlin?), use the carpet swatch that lines the bottom of your trunk.

Securely jam whatever you use under the front of the drive wheels. If your car is front-wheel drive, that means the front wheels, genius. If you're driving a four-wheel drive vehicle, put pads under every tire if you can, or at least the two rear tires.

Start the car and slowly roll it onto the pads. Drive forward until you're on solid ground or, if you encounter more mud, repeat the procedure.

If you can't find a pad to use, deflate the tires until they're about half filled. This should create enough drag for you to drive forward. But deflated tires are dangerous to drive on, so fill them up as soon as possible.

Change a Flat

You might change a handful of flat tires in your life, but when it needs to be done, it needs to be done right. Especially when it's some beautiful damsel in distress on the side of a cold, dark road. Master the simple technique of switching a bad tire for a good one, and you stand a chance of being her knight in shining armor (well, a little greasy from the tire work, but still shiny).

Make sure the car is turned off and the parking brake is on. The car should be positioned as far off the road as possible, with the flashers on (and using a road flare or two isn't a bad idea either). Pull the jack and spare out of the trunk and look for a solid mounting surface for the type of jack you're using. Some cars have a notch in the frame to accommodate the jack face. Most others require the jack be posted under a solid portion of the frame. Don't put it under the suspension, under an unstable part such as a door, or under any part of the drive train such as the engine or transmission.

Before you start jacking up the car, use the lug wrench to "break" the lug nuts that hold the tire on. Then jack it up and unscrew the nuts the rest of the way by hand. Remove the damaged tire and slide the spare into place on the lug bolts. Tighten the lug nuts hand-tight, and then crank them once with the wrench. Lower the car, and finish up by tightening the lug nuts securely. Always tighten the nuts in a star pattern, or crisscross if there are only four. Stow the gear and ruined tire, and you—and your damsel—are good to go.

Replace an Air Filter

Your car breathes. Its breath is a lot worse than yours (or maybe not), but it still needs to breathe. Like you, it takes in air, and that air needs to be filtered. Let's face it, you wouldn't want to be breathing crap kicked up off the road over a hundred miles, would ya?

That makes your car's air filter mighty important, even though it's one of the simplest pieces to check and replace. It's essential that you regularly check it because there's really no reliable way to know if the filter is so dirty it's not doing its job. Every car drives over different roads, in different conditions, all of which will radically affect how long a filter lasts.

Different cars and engines locate the filter in differ places, but on all cars, it's one of the easiest things to access and change. If you're driving a pre-'80s classic, your air filter will most likely be in a round metal container centered over the top of the engine, secured with a wing nut. Modern cars place the filter inside a plastic housing that's usually rectangular or square (it's generally the blockiest thing you see when you open your hood). The housing is opened by unlatching spring latches along one or both sides or, in rarer cases, unscrewing mounting screws.

Whatever the case, remove the filter and inspect it under bright light. Direct sunlight is best. It will be easy to see a dense layer of caked-on dirt. If this is the case, time to change the filter. Buy a new one (take the old one to check that the new matches exactly) and drop it into the housing after cleaning the housing's interior. Secure the cover, and get back on the road where you and your ride can breathe freely.

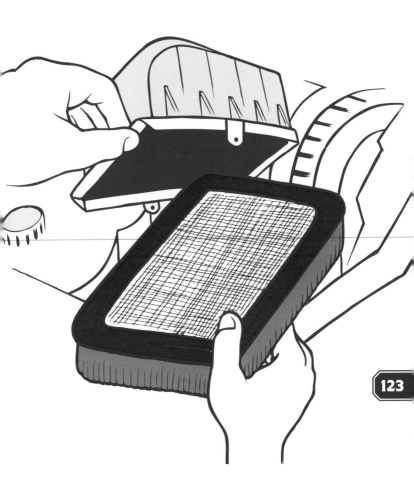

Survive a Skid

Doesn't matter if it happens because you hit a big patch of black ice, or simply because you were moving too quickly into that hairpin corner (so much for Speed Racer fantasies). Slamming into a skid will definitely test the limits of your blood pressure meds. Keep your wits about you and do the counterintuitive thing, and you will come out of this particular road-racing emergency just fine.

As long as you can stay calm, your chances of recovering control of your car are pretty good, depending on what's causing the skid. If you feel the front wheels come loose and glide, take your foot off the gas, but don't brake. Allow the car to decelerate and drift until the front wheels grab again. If you haven't flailed the wheel, you'll be headed in the direction you meant to go in the first place.

If the rear wheels—or all four—break loose, you'll feel the car glide and it's likely the rear end will start floating toward the front, as if you were doing a slow-motion donut. Lay off the brake and gas, and steer firmly into the skid (in the direction you're skidding) and wait for the wheels to grab. Depending on how much you've turned the wheel, the car may grab and skid in the opposite direction. In this case, steer back into the skid again. Be ready to straighten the wheel and point the car in the direction you want to go.

No matter what caused the skid, or what type of skid it is, looking where you want to go is going to increase your chances of eventually heading in that direction. Look at a pole, hit a pole. Once you get out of the skid successfully, head on home and change your trousers.

Car straightens out

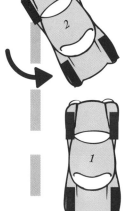

*Crank steering
wheel to the right*

*Rear wheels
skid right*

Car Skids

Lose a Tail

There it this: a black sedan following you. Indistinct driver, no plates. CIA? Friends of your bookie? There's no way to know. But this much is certain: you have to lose that tail.

First, confirm that it isn't just your meds wearing off and unreasonable paranoia taking over. Take three right turns. If the car is still in your rearview mirror, you're being followed.

To lose him, navigate into the left lane approaching a stoplight, so that you'll be in the front of the line (slowing down so you don't make the yellow is the way to do this). As the car to your right lane stops and cross-traffic starts, accelerate into a right turn ahead of cross-traffic. Your tail is now landlocked, waiting for the light to change. Accelerate to the next turn and disappear.

Manage a High-Speed Blowout

As automotive emergencies go, a blowout at highway speeds ranks up there with flames shooting out from the hood. When the blowout happens it's going to shake you up, because it's such a sudden, disconcerting event. Especially if it's a front tire, in which case the steering wheel will go wonky.

No sudden moves. Steer as steady as possible and—here's the odd part—stay on the accelerator. Unless it's completely shredded, the tire will stay moderately inflated at speed. It's just a matter of physics. Decelerate and it will flatten entirely.

Drive to a safe exit, such as a stretch of wide shoulder, long enough for you to slow down and come to a stop. Ease the car over—no sudden movements!—and bring it to a stop as far out of traffic as possible. Take a moment to consider yourself skilled; a lesser man would have probably rolled that sucker.

Stop the Car When Your Brakes Fail

When your car decides that a body in motion should stay in motion, you have a lot of decisions to make. Much of what you do depends on the situation. Driving down the freeway gives you more pondering time than if you're 50 feet from a red light. Regardless, quickly determine what type of brake failure it is. A soft pedal with barely any resistance points to a hydraulic problem. A solid, unmovable pedal is evidence of a mechanical problem or something wedged under the pedal. A pedal that drops to the floor means complete system failure.

This matters because a spongy brake pedal may come back to life with vigorous pumping. A frozen pedal may be freed by removing the blockage. If you can't quickly solve it though, decelerate the car any way you can. Step off the gas and downshift until you're in the lowest gear. Now it's time for plan B.

If you have a hand brake, hold the button down and pull the lever just hard enough to slow the car without skidding. If it's a foot brake, pull or push the release mechanism and stay on it while you engage the brake and slow the car.

Turn on your hazard lights and start honking. You should be able to stop the car with the parking brake, but if you can't, go to the nuclear option: find an immovable object. Gravel, wet grass or the deep wet soil of a wide median can slow things down. A steep hill on a turnoff can also bring the car to a gentle stop. Barring those options, use contact and friction. Plowing through dense shrubs or, short of landscaping, look for direct contact. Use whatever soft-yet-unyielding surface you can find. Remember the fighter pilot's motto: any landing you walk away from is a good landing.

Parallel Park with Ease

Driving entails many potentially cool moves, but one of the coolest is pulling up to a parking space along the curb between two cars, and smoothly backing your ride into it in one clean move. The art of parallel parking is all about spatial relationships, and is one of the most improbably difficult skills for drivers to master. But you are the master of all things automotive, so this is a trick that needs to be in your driving bag.

The maneuver is actually fairly simple; it's just a matter of getting your perception right. Use reference points to guide you.

Pull up next to the car in front of the space, so that the front of your car is two feet behind the front of the parked car. If you look to your right, you should be staring at the post between the car's driver's side front and back windows. Now look back, over your inside shoulder, while turning the wheel to the right. Turn it just enough to aim your car back into the spot. You should use your sight line to aim for the inside headlight of the car behind the parking space. Don't oversteer or you'll have to start over.

Straighten out the wheel just as your front bumper comes even with the front car's rear bumper. As soon as you are clear of the front car, crank the wheel to the left. Back in and straighten your front wheels out.

Do it right, and you will slide right into position. If you are in a tight space, or your aim was a little off, you may need to drive forward a little. With your car safely tucked into its resting spot, get out and resist the urge to admire your parking prowess. Nobody likes a showboat.

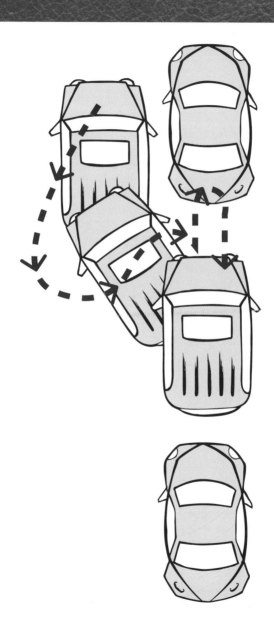

Avoid a Wreck

The absolute biggest drag in riding a motorcycle is dumping it. Even if you're lucky enough to walk away, it's no fun nursing a racing stripe of road rash. The best way to handle a motorcycle accident is not to have one. And that requires driving in a much different way than you would in a car.

First and foremost is road awareness. Cruising down the road in a big four-wheeled box, you can zone out and slip into "auto-pilot" every once in a while. But that don't fly if you're handling a relatively tiny two-wheeler. Cars and trucks inevitably misjudge your position, so you need to be ever vigilant. Constantly scan the road and vehicles ahead and to the sides of you. Regularly check your mirrors, but the front and sides are where sudden threats are going to come from. Watch the tires on vehicles to anticipate sudden, unsignaled lane changes, and watch through the windshields of cars in front of you for any problem stacking up that would require quick braking.

Be as visible as possible to other drivers. Wear bright clothing; better to look like a geek than die a fashion horse. Ride in the center of your lane, where you're less likely to be covered up by a driver's blind spot. Always signal lane changes so that other drivers know what to expect.

Last, and most importantly, always have an emergency exit plan. This means not letting traffic box you in. You can play it like a game. What happens if that minivan on the right veers into your lane? What if the overstacked boards in the bed of that pickup ahead come unbundled and spew themselves across the road? Know what action you'll take. Ultimately, anticipating trouble is your best way of avoiding becoming someone's hood ornament.

Kick Start a Motorcycle

It's a once in a lifetime chance, the opportunity to ride a classic chopper, or that pristine restored '60s Triumph your neighbor's been rebuilding for years. Don't blow it at the starting line. If you're looking for the electric starter, chances are the owner is going to shake his head, and gently remove you from his prize steel horse.

It is okay, however, to ask about the bike's particular starting sequence. It may have an ignition retard that needs to be switched on before starting. Classic Harleys usually need to be primed by kicking them over with the throttle held open, and then choked for the real start-up. Other bikes will simply need to be choked before starting—the basic for any bike that is kick-started.

Once you've prepped for ignition, put on your best pair of work boots and long pants, and flip out the kick lever. Lift up slightly, pause as you raise your leg to coil your body mass and then unload all your weight downward through the kickstart leg in a burst. Smaller bikes will fire right up or the lever will go loose under your weight. Some bigger bikes require that you keep your leg loose, because the kick lever can recoil with the engine's compression. A bigger engine's heavy compression is also why kickstarting something like a '48 Panhead requires that you come down on the lever with all your weight.

If you've kicked till your leg goes numb, there's a problem. If the bike hasn't been well maintained, it could be a worn magneto, although first make sure you've turned the gas tank valve to the "open" position. When the bike starts, let it idle to warm up, close the choke when it's warm, and head off on your dream ride, like Brando in *The Wild One*.

Ace a High-Speed Turn

What's the use of owning that tricked-out superbike if you can't open her up once in a while? Letting the monster loose on straightaways is easy, but taking a turn when you're moving at lightspeed is a matter of using physics to your advantage.

Understand that the tendency of a 300-pound bike screaming down a straight stretch of road is to keep going straight. You're going to have to convince it to change direction. The process is an event in three fluid parts: the entrance, holding the turn, and the exit.

As you approach to enter the turn, decelerate smoothly and modestly. At high speed, brakes heat up quickly and can fade with surprising suddenness. Downshifting and laying off the throttle are better ways of controlling your entrance speed. Knowing the right speed to enter a corner is a matter a practice, which you should have plenty of before going full speed.

Once you're inside the turn, you'll be using your body as a counterweight to the centrifugal forces that want to pull the bike out of the turn. Trust your tires and lean the bike into the turn. Depending on how fast you're going, you'll need to slide off the seat and adopt the classic racer's pose: inside thigh straddling the seat, butt hanging off a few inches, and your inside leg forming a triangle with the point—the knee—hanging just above the asphalt.

Hold the turn with your lower body in this position. You can shift your upper body to fine tune the lean of the bike and make corrections as you hold the turn, if it feels like the bike is pulling out early. Exit the turn smoothly, letting the bike come upright, sliding back into the seat, and accelerating into the next straightaway.

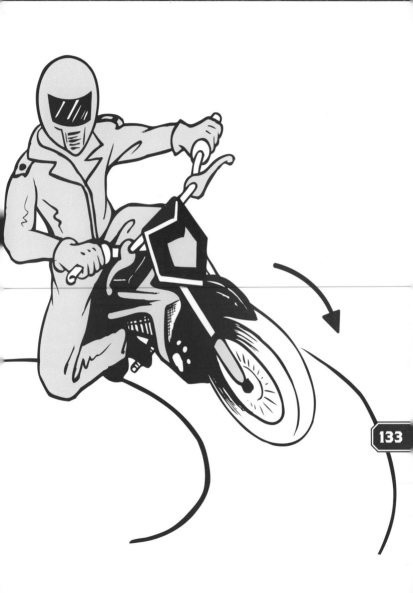

133

Pick Up a Dropped Bike

There's something particularly disheartening about seeing your bike lying on its side. It's plainly unnatural. It's even more disconcerting when it's on its side because you dumped. But whether it fell over in the garage, or you dropped it going around a tight curve, you need to quickly get the bike back on its feet again before fluid starts draining or you get caught in the road. And you want to pick it up without popping a hernia or damaging your back.

Make sure the bike is turned off before you try to raise it upright. Then, like your gym coach always told you, lift with your legs. A full-dresser touring bike can weigh upwards of 600 pounds and even a streamlined crotch rocket can run north of 300 pounds. Lifting that much weight the wrong way is a sure formula for dropping the bike again and causing further damage, or injuring your back in ways you don't want to injure your back.

To lift the bike without damage to you or it, lock the handlebars (if you have a handlebar lock). Then squat low with your lower back against the lower edge of the seat, at about the middle of the bike. Grab ahold of a fixed, solid piece of the frame or bike on either side, and begin to straighten your legs. Work slowly, keep your back straight and head up, and lever upwards, not back (you could wind up just sliding the thing along). Take small steps and continue walking the bike upright, until it's in riding position. Make sure you're stable, and slowly turn and straddle the bike. Put down the kickstand and rest before continuing on your way (which will probably lead you down the road, to the motorcycle dealer where you'll trade for a smaller, lighter model).

CHAPTER № 5

Emergency!

YOU DON'T NEED A RED CAPE AND FANCY TIGHTS TO BE the hero of the hour (although it doesn't hurt). You just need to be a man who can keep thinking while others panic, and who isn't afraid to take action and risk a little for the greater good. That's all you, isn't it?

The truth is, calmness is not the baseline for most people in an emergency. They usually become unnerved and freeze. Or worse, they get in the way and complicate the crisis. Be different from the crowd by equipping yourself with the modest knowledge it takes to handle most emergencies. Having that knowledge will make it even easier to stay calm and in control.

The pages that follow will prepare you for those rare occasions when someone gets himself in the kind of trouble he can't get out of, and needs someone else to get his back. The man who grabs his chest and falls over, or the gal who finds herself stuck in a car with a downed power line draped across the hood. They all need your help, and you'll find the way to do that in this chapter. Be the Manskills rescue man. It's your destiny.

On occasion, to be the rescuer means to put aside a few qualms about your own safety (after all, what endangers others often endangers rescuers) and the squeamishness that caused you to turn off TLC's open heart surgery special. But look, if it were easy, everyone would remain stoically calm in every situation, and they'd all know what to do no matter what the circumstance. That's one of the things that make the Manskill man—he doesn't flinch in the face of difficult things. He trusts himself.

You can escape the fire and lead others to safety. You can free the stuck kid, and save the knocked-out tooth and treat that snakebite. You can handle any situation because you have the power of Manskills behind you. You may not have the cape, but you'll have the confidence of your inner hero. Taller than the tallest buildings and stronger than a speeding locomotive, right, pal?

Save a Choker

Don't be a spectator when your best buddy swallows a fist-size piece of steak and it stops halfway down. Simple choking can escalate into a life-threatening condition in seconds. You're going to want to get his back, literally.

That said, take care not to rush in prematurely. A person can often clear his own throat. If your wingman can still speak or make noise, air is flowing and you need to let nature take its course. If his face goes beet red and he goes silent, it's definitely time to do your thing.

Get someone to call 911 (better to look stupid than be a pall bearer). Stand to the side and a little behind him (get him standing too) and cinch his gut so that he bends over slightly. Using the heel of your hand, deliver five solid blows right between his shoulder blades. Don't worry about hurting him; this is his life we're talking about.

Most of the time, the blows will clear the airway. But sometimes, it will take a bit more effort to get him breathing again. If he continues to choke, pull a Heimlich by getting behind him and circling you arms around his torso. Make a fist with the thumb pointed in and position it right at your patient's belly button. Grab the outside of the fist with the other hand.

Now pull toward yourself with a sudden jerk so that you're compressing into the chest cavity. Repeat several times. Chances are you'll clear the airway. If you don't, and the ambulance hasn't arrived yet, you're probably going to need to do some CPR (page 144). Mouth to mouth. While that is certain to test the limits of your friendship, just think about how big he is going to owe you.

First Option: A blow between the shoulder blades

Second Option: The Heimlich Maneuver

Save Someone From Drowning

You don't have to be a lifeguard to make a rescue in the water. You just have to recognize signs of trouble and be a fairly strong swimmer.

A drowning person will look far different from someone who's just gracelessly struggling to swim. Telltale signs include the person fighting to keep her head above water, flailing her arms, and an inability to stay afloat. You're not going to have a lot of time; if you think she may be in trouble, start swimming toward her. If she tells you to go away, no harm, no foul.

Grab any possible floatation device—a life preserver, life jacket, or even one of those bright orange floats real lifeguards use. It may seem like a pain to swim with, but it'll help when you reach the victim. If anybody else is around, ask them to call 911.

Swim straight at the person, keeping her in view. Unless she actually slips below the surface, in which case keep your eye on the spot you last saw her. That will be your dive-down location.

When you reach the person, she'll be freaking. Position yourself behind her. Drowning victims are often so panicked that they slap a death grip on their rescuer, dragging the poor soul down. Loop your arms under her armpits. If you've got a floating device, jam it between the two of you if she's flailing, or let her hold onto it if she's calm. Use your free arm to start stroking back to shore or to the nearest boat.

Once you get the person on land or in a craft, get her under a blanket and check for signs that she swallowed a lot of water. Any person who has come close to drowning should be checked out by emergency medical personnel.

Free a Child's Head Stuck Between Bars

Kids. If there is a way to turn something totally benign into something dangerous, they'll find it. To a kid, staircase balusters are jailer's bars, through which a head needs to go.

Problem is, once a kid's head has been contorted to go through the impossibly tiny space between balusters, the International Law of Bizarro Physics states there shall be no easy way to reverse the process. Be the good uncle and defy that law.

You could grease the little tyke's head with shampoo, soap, or another slippery substance. But that rarely works, and in the meanwhile, the child will start to panic, realizing he has gotten himself into a serious pickle and may spend the rest of his days as some kind of banister freak, laughed at and derided by former school chums and family alike. The parents often follow suit, picturing the glowering accusatory faces of the child protective services enforcers.

Curtail all that tomfoolery by working on the bars. If the bars are wood, cut one at top and bottom to free the child. The baluster can be replaced with a little work, but a child on the verge of meltdown is not so easily fixed.

If the rails in question are metal, get your hands on a long pry bar (crow bar, barbell pole, etc.) and pry the bars apart slightly, just enough to allow safe removal of the head. Two adult men may even be able to create enough separation by pulling on the bars. If neither solution works, find an expandable, accordion-style tire jack, collapse it all the way, place it sideways between the bars, and crank it open until the head slides free.

Move an Injured Person

Remember the code, real man: Never leave someone behind. Sometimes the injured just have to be moved, and sometimes it's up to you to move them. Of course, if the victim has sustained a serious spinal injury, you'll want to move them only if you absolutely have to, to save their life.

You have two options: lifting and carrying, or crafting an emergency stretcher. Carry a person by yourself in the "fireman's" carry (duck and pick him up as he faces you so that his waist is resting on your shoulder).

Enlist the aid of bystander and you'll have more options. Make what is known as a "pack saddle" by grabbing your right wrist with your left hand to form an L. The carrier across from you does the same and you grab each other's left wrist with your free right hands, to form a square seat. The injured person rides, but must be conscious.

Carry an unconscious person by facing the other carrier, and both of you grabbing the opposite person's wrist and shoulder (left to right in both cases). This creates a cradle in which an unconscious person lays.

You can also create a stretcher to drag alone or carry between two people. You need two handles, roughly six feet long. Solid tent poles, branches, or cot rails will do. Spread out a blanket and divide the blanket lengthwise into thirds, by placing the handles across the blanket, one-third the length from each end. Now fold the outside left third over to the right, and the outside right third over the left. Lay the person on top, and his weight will hold the blanket in place. As an alternative, you can thread the handles through a sturdy shirt (buttoned if it's a button-up style) or through the legs of pants.

Perform CPR

The bad news: stunning Victoria Secret models rarely collapse, lying motionless in dire need of a long round of cardiopulmonary resuscitation. The worst news: It's usually the overweight guy in the corner, the one with the skin condition and bad breath, who grabs his chest and drops like a stone, in dire need of a long round of cardiopulmonary resuscitation. The good news: save that guy's life by keeping his heart going until it can beat on its own or help arrives, and you have just added a big long row of bricks to your mansion in heaven.

The actual process of CPR is fairly simple. When someone collapses and stops breathing, call 911. Then go to work. First off, begin chest compressions. Put whatever hand you write with in the middle of his chest, fingers splayed. Put your other hand on top and interlock your digits. Keep your elbows locked and thrust down, compressing the chest 2 inches—you may feel some snapping and popping, but keep it up in a steady rhythm. If you've never been trained in the CPR process, the American Heart Association recommends you limit your efforts to compressing the chest until help arrives, or the person regains consciousness.

If you have been trained, you know to check his breathing after 30 chest compressions. Determine if any air is going in an out, check his airway for obstructions and remove any you find. Then tilt his head back and lift his chin. Pinch off his nostrils so that they are entirely closed, and put your mouth covering his (yes, dude, really). Breathe deep into his mouth, with two separate breaths. Grossed out? C'mon pal, you've kissed worse. If he doesn't come back to the land of the living, start 30 more chest compressions, and repeat.

Use a Fire Extinguisher

Ah, the fire extinguisher. Such a reassuring presence, as if the mere fact of a fire extinguisher mounted nearby might prevent a dangerous blaze in the first place.

Were it only true. In fact, a fire extinguisher can be a false sense of security. Especially if you've never bothered to figure out how it works. Because as sure as the swallows return to Capistrano each year, you won't have much luck with an extinguisher if the first time you consider its operation is when a fire has broken out.

Know what type it is. Extinguishers are rated A, B, or C, for the class of fire they fight (respectively: wood and paper, flammable liquids like grease, and electrical fires). Most homes are best served by a multi-class extinguisher rated ABC.

When facing a fire, judge whether it's actually worth fighting. Generally, if half a room is in flames, it's too late for an extinguisher. In fact, if the fire is bigger than you, firefighters generally recommend calling 911 and getting you and anybody else out and away from the fire.

If you deem it manageable, remember the acronym "PASS." PASS stands for Pull, Aim, Squeeze, Sweep. Pull the pin for the handle, which may entail breaking glass or snapping a seal to get at the pin itself. Aim the nozzle at the base of the fire. Then squeeze the trigger to start the chemical blast. Sweep the extinguisher's spray side to side across the fire's base. Keep sweeping and blasting until the fire is out.

If you've had a fire that required full extinguishing, it's important to call the fire department to inspect the area and ensure you have no hidden hot spots. You don't want Mr. Flame rearing his ugly head after you've already used up your extinguisher.

Ride Out an Earthquake

Earthquakes are always a bit of a surprise. If you already live in an earthquake-prone area, you've no doubt set aside the requisite earthquake kit complete with basic tools, first aid supplies, the minimum of water and food for at least a week, blankets, flashlight, batteries, and a portable radio. Your first concern when the rumbler hits is keeping yourself out of harm's way.

The ideal place to be is where nothing can fall on you. The middle of a football field is ideal. Unfortunately, it's hard to plan your location around an earthquake. So, you might be in your car. Pull off the road as far away from telephone poles, overpasses, power lines, and buildings as possible. Stay in your car; it affords some measure of protection against falling debris. Stay there until you're absolutely sure the quake and aftershocks are over.

More than likely, however, you'll be in a building. Get clear of the structure if there is a large, open space next to it. Otherwise, get as far away from the windows as possible, and seek shelter under the sturdiest piece of furniture you can find. During the earthquake, stay on your knees with your head and neck covered by your hands and arms. If you're outside, stay away from power lines, poles, and anything else that could fall on you.

Afterward, exercise caution. Assess whether your structure is safe. Aftershocks are just about guaranteed, and a strong one can bring down a damaged structure. Check the building for spot fires, gas leaks (you'll know by the smell), and obvious damage that indicates the structure is compromised. Also check for electrical problems—anything sparking means shutting off the power to the whole building.

In your car, tune to the local emergency broadcast station for information about road conditions. After all, before you head off anywhere, you want to be sure you can get there.

Survive a Flash Flood

We all like a good swim now and again, but not when you're lying in your tent after a day of hiking, you're out walking your dog, or you're just driving to the store. But that's how quick the watery demon of a flash flood can strike. The defining characteristics of this nasty natural disaster is how quick and hard it hits.

The worst place to be is in your car. You'll see the flooding happen—it occurs in a flash after all—and at first sign leave your car. Don't worry about the vehicle being waterlogged, you can let the insurance company sort it out (it's a lot better than finding out how good your death benefits are). Over half of flash flood fatalities happen in vehicles. And most of those occur because people mistakenly drive across what they think is just a shallow eddy. But the current is running so quick and hard, that it carries the vehicle to deeper waters.

Outside your vehicle, getting through a flash flood unscathed is largely a matter of position. If you find yourself in a low-lying area, downstream of dam, or nearby a riverbank, find higher ground. If you're in your home, head to the roof. This is one time when it's not only legal, but smart to get high.

No matter what, fight the urge to swim after your belongings or even your pets. The fast-moving water of a flash flood—shallow or not—is so strong that it can sweep away even a strong swimmer. Your whole goal should be to stay out of the water.

Once the flood is over, stay where you are. Rescuers generally do a grid-by-grid search for survivors, and your chances of being quickly found are better if you're visible and stationary.

Drive with a Popped Hood

It's easy to take the clear view through your windshield for granted. But when your hood pops up, you start to appreciate just how valuable it is to see the road.

Shock and awe aside, this emergency is really not all that serious.

Keep driving until you can safely and sanely pull to the side of the road. Ignore your high-triple-digit heart rate, and either look through the open space at the base of your windshield, or stick your head out the driver's side window to steer. This will give you plenty of visibility and a chance to get the car off the road without further incidence.

Once you've stopped as far off the road as possible, check that the hood can be relatched, and that it is solidly held down. If the latch is tentative, damaged, or the hood itself is visibly warped or misshapen, call for a tow.

Outlast a Tornado

Even with today's sophisticated weather tracking technology, the science of predicting when and where a tornado will strike (or move) is still pretty imprecise. And unfortunately, even a near-miss can be catastrophic. If you see a tornado, gauge its movement. Pick a landmark to the left or right and note if it gets closer or farther away from the landmark. Whatever way the tornado is moving, you need to gun it in the opposite direction if you are in your car. If you're not in your car or the tornado is gaining on you faster than you can move, seek shelter. Your car is not shelter. An underground tornado shelter would be wonderful, but what are the odds? Next up is a deep basement, preferably one with no windows. If there are windows, block them with anything solid you can find. No basement? Get to the lowest floor of the building and cover yourself with anything soft, like a mattress or a dense layer of thick blankets. Now just wait.

Survive an Avalanche

Mother Nature has her temper tantrums, but few are as purely terrifying as a full-blown avalanche. The best course of action is prevention. Stay off backcountry slopes of 35 to 45 degrees and away from tree-stripped alleys that indicate a previous avalanche route. If you must hike on snow-covered mountain terrain, attach an avalanche beacon to an inner layer of clothing. In an emergency, the beacon will emit a signal that rescuers can follow to find you under the snow.

An avalanche announces itself with a thunder-like boom. The snow pack will be traveling in excess of 60 miles an hour, so you're not going to directly outrun it. Instead, if you have a viable escape route off to the side, take it.

If you're trapped in an avalanche's path, ditch equipment and supplies because you want to be as light as possible. Crouch down to limit your body target area because fully half of the avalanche deaths each year are the result of blunt force trauma from debris in snow.

The avalanche has the same wave effect as a strong surf. Get as close to the surface as possible. Swim as hard you can—the entire event usually takes less than a minute. As you come to rest, make a space as large as possible with your hands in front of your face. This will create an air pocket, which is vitally important because the snow settles and hardens into a dense layer in the aftermath of the avalanche. If you're very close to the surface, slowly dig an access hole. Otherwise, conserve oxygen by remaining calm. Don't shout for help unless you can hear rescuers moving over the snow; the packed snow will usually mute any noise. Your fate is now in the hands of the rescuers. After you're extricated, it's time to consider summer sports.

Right a Capsized Canoe

Canoes are prone to tip over and they can be downright flummoxing to turn right side up again. And then there's the daunting challenge of getting back in once you've managed to turn the thing right side up.

It's all a matter of balance. If you're on a river, gather everything that was thrown out of the canoe and pop it under the overturned canoe. Then swim the canoe to the nearest shore. Once on land, turn the canoe over and shove off as you would anywhere.

In the middle of a lake or a bigger river, a capsized canoe is a bit more of a challenge. You'll be aided by your life jacket, which will keep you afloat while you gather your energy for the righting. Slide the paddles under the canoe, and follow them. There will be an air pocket, allowing you to breathe and initiate the first part of the project: righting the canoe.

Position yourself at the center and grab the side that to which you'll be righting the boat. Now put your other hand on the center seat or centerboard support, dip down and then scissor kick as powerfully upward as you can. When you pop up out of the water, jerk the side of the boat down at the same time you give the center seat a mighty shove. The canoe should flip over if you've done the push-pull motion hard enough. It may take a couple of tries. Rest between tries, but not too long—cold water may steal your energy and put you at risk of hypothermia.

Righting the canoe is always easier with two people, as is getting back in.

With the canoe sitting right-side up in the water, it's time to get back in the boat. If you have a partner, position one of you on either side of the boat. While one person gets in, the other will steady the side. Then the person inside the boat counterbalances the weight to allow the person in the water to come up over the side.

The same mounting motion is used whether you're alone or in pairs, but you'll just have to do it more carefully if you're by yourself.

Position yourself at the middle of the canoe's length. Grab the edge and get ready to kick up and out of the water as high as you can. Explode out of the water and throw your free hand across to grab the other side. Simultaneously curve your torso over the near edge and fluidly turn your body so that you land in the bottom butt first. Keep your center of gravity low and controlled throughout. All that remains is to paddle away.

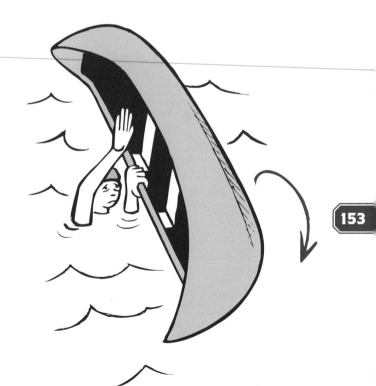

Deal with a Downed Power Line

You might be the type of guy who can lift two five-gallon pails of paint like they were marshmallow fluff, and laughs off the kind of suture-worthy injuries that would send lesser models of manhood skittering to the emergency room. All this may be so. But you will never win a confrontation with Mr. Electricity. Especially not in the concentrated form that flows through a high voltage power line.

Caution has never been more important than when you come across a downed power line, or one comes across you. If a power line falls on a car you're in, stay inside. The car is grounded and you're not. Don't touch anything inside the car. Just breathe easy and wait for the professionals to arrive and bail you out.

Generally, downed power lines are to be avoided. Never assume that one is not live simply because it's not doing the movie thing and sparking like some Fourth of July fireworks display. If you feel you absolutely have to get around the wire, be aware the electricity can be conducted along the surface of a water puddle, grease in the road, or any other conductive surface like a metal plate. Always best to go back the way you came whenever possible.

Of course, you may have come across a victim of that power line. Do the right thing, but don't get killed doing it. Get the person away from the power line with whatever wooden object is at hand. A chair, a broomstick or even a branch will serve. Under no circumstances should you touch the victim until he is well away from the wire. When you have him safely in hand, check the victim for a pulse and determine if he is breathing. If not, start CPR.

Fix Frostbite

You don't have to be a braniac to know the downside to winter sports is the cold. More than simple discomfort, low temperatures can lead to the very unpleasant and appendage-threatening condition called frostbite.

Frostbite happens in stages, and the earlier you catch it, the easier it is to remedy. It starts with a tingling sensation almost like when a foot goes to sleep. The skin numbs up and takes on an unusual, waxy texture. At the other end of the spectrum the skin is actually, black and completely cold to the touch, and chances are the affected area isn't going to make it as part of your body much longer.

The solution is simple and a little obvious: you need to heat up the affected area. But this can be easier said than done in the great outdoors and, in any case, you need to be careful how you warm up your frostbitten parts. If you can, get to shelter and start quaffing warm water or warm tea. Get your frostbitten part under dry warm blankets or clothes and let your body do the warming. Go slow. Trying to heat frostbitten skin under hot water or by rubbing vigorously can hurt as much as it helps.

You'll know when the frostbite is being conquered because the skin will start to have sensation again. That sensation may be a little unpleasant at first, almost like burning, depending how severe the frostbite was, but that's the healing process. In any case, if you've experienced any prolonged changes in skin color and texture, or if the skin remains numb, you need to get a medical pro on the case as soon as possible. Even moderate frostbite can lead to lasting damage and requires a professional medical assessment.

Bust Down a Door

Let's assume, for argument's sake, that you need to bust down a door to save someone from a fire, and not that you want to get into your girlfriend's house to catch her with the other man. Better to stick to the high road.

Don't even consider ramming it with your shoulder. Your shoulder is a very complicated joint that was not built to withstand direct impact. A door, generally speaking, was. Two guesses which one of those comes away from the meeting in better shape. Keep your shoulder to yourself and use basic physics instead.

Before you go all Rambo on the door, first check to see if it's even locked. Next, look at the hinges. If the door opens outward, even Sgt. Fury couldn't get through it without a battering ram and a half hour of hard labor. In other words, if opens toward you, you'll need to find a window or a small amount of C4.

If the door is ripe for breeching, you'll need to generate the most force possible. Plant your non-kick foot slightly behind your body as a solid base, cock your kicking leg, and then explode through your hips, putting all your weight into the kick. You want to kick with your heel, aiming to the inside of the door handle, or deadbolt if there is one. Don't actually kick the hardware; that's just a recipe for injury.

Depending on what the door is made of and how sturdy the deadbolt is, it's likely that you'll need more than one kick. But even if the door is solid, the jamb is probably wood. Sooner or later, one of the two will splinter into pieces and give way. Then you're clear to save those kittens from the fire. Sgt. Fury would be proud.

Cut Off a Limb to Save Your Life

Hands, arms, and legs are all pretty nifty parts of the machine called your body. But sometimes you have to choose the whole team over one member. If you're stuck in the wrong place, held fast by a pinned limb, it may have to go.

But first, exhaust all other options. If you have enough food and water to hold out, wait for rescuers to find you. Use a rope, hiking pole, ski, or other prying implement to free the limb. Even if you damage it, better a broken wing than no wing at all.

Sometimes, though, removal is the only answer. Use a sharp instrument such as a hunting knife or a multipurpose tool blade. Even the sharp edge of a large flat piece of shale or scree can work.

Apply a tourniquet, using shoelaces, a T-shirt or anything else that can be tied around the limb, between the amputation point and the body. Tie it super tight. This is very important.

Start slicing. Put your belt between your teeth and cut cleanly and quickly around the limb and down to the bone. You'll feel the blade contact bone, and then make a cut all around it.

Now break through the bone. You won't be able to cut through it even with a very sharp edge. You can smash the bone with a large rock or other heavy implement, but if possible, use your knife to score a reasonably clean fracture line. Depending on where you're stuck and the angle of your body, you may be able to lever the limb, to crack the bone in the question.

If you've managed to power through this without fainting, you are indeed special forces material. But the ordeal is not yet over.

Sever any remaining tissue. Dress the stump as best you can. Get to medical help as fast as humanly possible.

Handle a Severed Appendage

Looking at a severed digit is disconcerting. Your initial reaction may be to lose your lunch, but buck up because there's every chance that the body part can be put back where it belongs. The key to success is getting it to the operating room in optimal condition.

First things first though. Call 911. Professional expertise will be essential if the victim goes into shock, and EMTs will also be well-versed in transporting severed digits.

Stop the bleeding at the amputation site, and dress the stub with sterile gauze. Gently wash the severed part without scrubbing or even rubbing, and wrap in dampened sterile gauze. Place the unit in a dry sandwich bag, and place that plastic bag in another bag filled with ice.

Even if you decide, for whatever reason, to take off for the emergency room before the ambulance arrives, drive sane. The part can be successfully reattached hours after the initial injury.

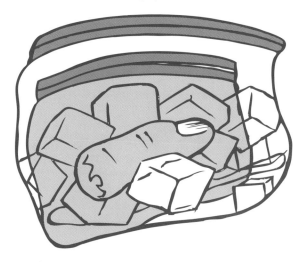

Survive a Freefall Elevator

The worst of all possible outcomes in an elevator is that the down button is taken literally. Terrifying as a freefall might be, you're not likely to die; elevator technology ensures that the only type that can descend in freefall are hydraulic versions that can't go higher than 70 feet. (The reason why this particular emergency is extremely rare.)

Focus on limiting damage. Lie face down at the center of the floor with your arms covering the back of your head. This position will distribute the impact over the greatest amount of body surface. You're also in a position to defend yourself against debris from the elevator crumpling. Don't buy into the urban myth that you can jump at just the right moment and come out of the incident unscathed. It's impossible to time a jump that precisely.

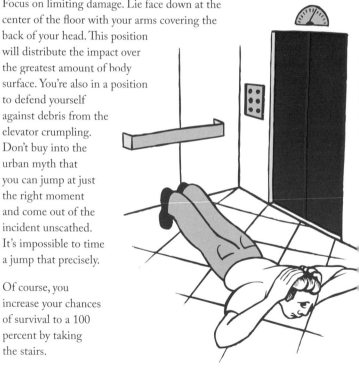

Of course, you increase your chances of survival to a 100 percent by taking the stairs.

EMERGENCY! ☞ Managing Chaos

Finesse Food Poisoning

We've all done it. Halfway through the afternoon, blood sugar waning dangerously, and the only food source around for blocks is the street vendor selling oddly gray hot dogs. But it's just a hot dog. What could be the harm?

Pity the poor soul who can answer that question in detail.

Food poisoning is the result of bacteria growth due to improper food preparation or handling. (It should have been a tip off when the hot dog vendor snatched the dog from the bin with his fingers . . .) The symptoms of real food poisoning are quick and definitive. You'll be evacuating at both ends, experiencing cramps when you're not, and generally feeling truly miserable for the entire ride. The secret to getting over a case of food poisoning is to avoid exacerbating the situation, and resetting your system.

Even though you want a cure (or simply to be put out of your misery), take it slow. Don't eat or drink anything for a couple of hours, until your stomach has completely calmed down. When time has passed, slowly introduce water, and electrolyte fluids like sports drinks to replace what vomiting has taken out of you. This won't immediately make you feel better, but it will set the stage for full recovery.

Next, introduce your system to the BRAT diet used with ailing children—bananas, rice, applesauce, and toast. Simple foods, gentle on the stomach. Ease in to normal foods after a day or so, when you're feeling more like yourself. Even though you may feel like you're on death's front door, you only need a doctor if you notice blood in vomit, experience a seizure or high fever, or fall victim to other, more severe symptoms. Otherwise, there's no speeding up the process. It's just a long trip through unhappyville.

Treat a Snakebite

Sneaky snakes rank right up there as nature's top buzz-killers (not to mention man-killers). Meet a snake on your way to a riverside picnic and your first indication is likely to be the sudden pain at the bite site.

Hopefully you'll get a glance at your attacker. Most snakes you'll come across aren't venomous; chances are good that you don't have poison coursing through your veins. But even if you are bitten by a venomous species, that doesn't necessarily mean the snake injected you with venom. Sometimes they bite "dry." Note the markings on the snake.

The two primary types of venomous North American snakes are pit vipers, a group that includes cottonmouths, copperheads, and rattlesnakes, and coral snakes. You'll know a pit viper by its characteristic triangular head and slit pupils. Both rattlesnakes and copperheads vibrate their tails before they strike, and the coppermouth shows the white interior of its mouth before biting.

Coral snakes are as beautiful as they are deadly. Their bodies are covered with bands of red, black, and yellow rings, and they have black noses. Sort of like the devil if he were a Mardi Gras boa. It's important to identify your attacker, because if it's poisonous, you'll want to get some anti-venom in you.

You'll probably notice swelling, pain, and bruising at the bite location, but headache and vomiting may follow. Don't try to suck the venom out (what are we, in a 1940s western?). Apply ice to ease the swelling and use ibuprofen for the pain.

In any case, if you are unsure or know for a fact that the snake is venomous, get to an emergency room. Based on your description of the snake and the symptoms you present, the doctor will decide a course of treatment, including whether or not you need anti-venom.

Treat a Sting

Sometimes a simple backyard barbecue can leave you feeling like a pincushion. Put yourself in the wrong place at the wrong time and bees, wasps and other sting-equipped warriors will see you as one big fleshy target.

In most cases, the stings these flying attackers lay on you are more a nuisance than a health problem. Basic triage for a single sting includes removing a stinger if one is stuck in your skin (bees are normally the only insects that leave their stingers behind). Put a cold pack on localized swelling, and smear on some hydrocortisone cream or calamine lotion. A dose of Benedryl will help with any mild allergic reactions like a larger rash and puffy eyes.

Sometimes, though, a small sting—or multiple stings—can set off a more serious allergic reaction, requiring immediate medical attention. The key is to be on the lookout for signs that point to a bigger problem and take them seriously. These include nausea, hives, a rash at the sting site that spreads to more than 2 inches in diameter, dizziness and extreme lightheadedness, a racing heartbeat, or any trouble breathing. Waste no time because a severe allergic reaction can spiral out of control quickly. Call 911 and administer epinephrine from an Epipen if whoever was stung is carrying it due to a previous anaphylactic reaction. Help the victim lie quietly inside, away from any possibility of further stings, until EMTs arrive. Don't be tempted to jump in the car and drive off in search of the hospital. Emergency medical personnel have everything they need to begin treatment the moment they arrive. However, keep a very close watch on the victim because you may have to start CPR if things go from bad to worse before help arrives.

Remove a Fishhook

Chase scaly prey long enough and you're bound to be skewered on your own sword. Putting a fishhook through a finger is one of those simple, non-life-threatening conditions that can still make you queasy. Use wire snips to snip off the line end of the hook and push it through in the direction of the barb. But this entails two holes. If the barb is hooked below the skin, there is a more ingenious solution.

Tie a loop of fishing line around the bend of the hook, and keep the line taut. Now push the end opposite the barb down so that it touches the skin. Yank the fishing line straight back and the barbed hook will exit the same way it went in.

Clean the wound thoroughly and cover it with antibacterial ointment. Protect it with a field dressing and check that your tetanus shots are up to date.

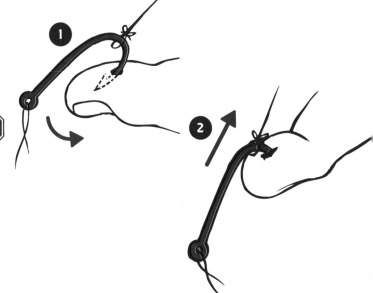

Treat a Burn

Not all burns are created equal. There's the got-a-splash-of-boiling-radiator-water-on-my-forearm burn, and then there's the caught-my-shirt-on-fire-with-the-welding-torch burn. Big difference. And they require different approaches to treatment.

That's why the medical know-it-alls classify burns as one of three levels of seriousness, from the relatively benign first degree, to extremely serious third degree. The seriousness is also compounded by the amount of surface area the burn covers. First-degree burns are surface level only, and generally superficial. They leave red skin in their wake, and nothing more. All you really need to do is run cold water over them to take away some of the sting, and pop a couple of Advil with copious amounts of water (dehydration from the burn combined with pain relievers can cause kidney problems).

The second-degree variety of burns cause blisters. The burn will be wet and will hurt to touch. A light washing of soap and water is the first step of treatment. After the burn is dry, cover it with a patch of sterile gauze and go see a doctor to ensure that infection isn't an issue (he may give you some antibiotic ointment to ward off infection). Ultimately, you may be looking at a little scarring.

Third-degree burns are the worst of the bunch. All of the skin has been burned away in areas, along with nerves, so that those areas are not painful. The burned areas may be open wounds, exposing underlying tissue to infection and further damage. The situation is a true medical emergency requiring specialized care to head off life-threatening infections, extreme shock, and to deal with what may be massive and ugly scarring. Much as you'd like to walk it off (you're a man, after all) a quick trip via ambulance is the only proper approach to third-degree burns.

Stop a Bleeding Wound

We are all just big sacks of blood. Open a deep gash while slipping down a rock face and it can seem like the dam that holds a great red river has broken. You need to stop that river from flowing.

The way to do that is pressure. Use a clean cloth or sterile gauze on the wound, but lacking anything sanitary, use whatever's on hand, including your hand. Press down as hard as possible. Forget the pain; blood is life and if you lose too much of it, well, you do the math.

The flow should stop within seconds. Elevate the wound physically higher than the victim's heart. Once the bleeding has stopped, apply a field dressing and get to the emergency room so a pro can have a look and stitch it up.

Deal with a Seizure

Seizures ain't pretty. Most people have a hard time even watching one. But think about it from the victim's perspective. Then minimize the potential danger of the surroundings.

Make sure anything that could hurt the victim is moved out of range. Other than that, there's not much you can or should do. Trying to hold down a seizure victim or, worse yet, putting something between his teeth, is actually counterproductive and can cause greater injury.

Once the seizure is over, make the victim comfortable. He will be disoriented and embarrassed. Tell him what happened, and offer assistance. A first-time seizure, a series of seizures, or a seizure that lasts several minutes merit a call to 911. But if the person is epileptic or has a history of seizures, he may not need emergency care. He can make that decision.

Beat Heat Stroke

Digging out that new pond by hand is manly. Getting red-faced and dizzy and passing out isn't manly. Heat stroke certainly isn't a manly thing. So steer clear of it with a few simple measures to be used anytime you're exerting yourself with the thermometer over 90.

Hydrate. Drink lots of fluids before, during, and after the activity. Avoid beverages containing sugar, alcohol, or caffeine, and very cold drinks.

Don't overdo. Exceeding your natural limits of endurance raises your body's core temperature, resulting in heat exhaustion and, if you continue, heat stroke. Take regular breaks in a cool garage, basement, or air-conditioned house.

Dress for success. Wear loose clothes, in breathable fabrics and light colors. These allow for the greatest amount of cooling ventilation and the least absorption of heat.

Know the signs of trouble. Heat exhaustion shows itself in a pale, washed-out skin tone, dizziness, nausea, and, as the condition progresses, vomiting and fainting. Your temperature will be somewhat high, around 101. You can't "power through" these symptoms. Instead, power down by hitting the couch with a plentiful supply of cool (not cold) water or sports drinks, a moist, cold towel on your head, and air conditioning or a fan on full blast.

Of course, you may have disregarded the initial signs of heat exhaustion and moved on to the more serious heat stroke. In this case, you'll be flushed, with hot and red skin, dizziness, a rapid pulse, and shallow breathing. You won't be sweating anymore (your body's doing everything it can to conserve fluids) and your temperature will be around 105 or higher. This is what is known as an extreme medical emergency. Do not take any aspirin or other drugs, alcohol or beverages other than water. Be smart, manly, and get to a hospital.

Splint a Broken Bone

Two-hundred eighty some odd bones in the body. That's a whole lot of chances to break one. If you give in to the odds and fracture a part of your skeleton, it's wise to immobilize. Keep the broken bone secure until you can get an X-ray and have an expert look it over, and you limit further damage.

Protect a break with a splint, the most basic of first aid devices. A splint is simply two or more rigid pieces bound to the injured limb to protect the break from direct impact or torsional forces that could make it worse. Obviously, splints are just for limb breaks—you don't splint a broken collarbone, ribs, or skull.

The rigid pieces can be just about anything. In the woods, two sturdy branches will do. Thick cardboard (or multiple layers) folded into a U makes a great impromptu splint. Boards and even metal rods will all do in a pinch.

There's very little to making the actual splint. The key is to immobilize: the splint should cover the joint before and after the break. Bind the rigid pieces of the splint with adhesive tape, duct tape, torn pieces of a shirt, plastic ties, or any other material that can be knotted and wound around the limb to hold the rigid splint pieces in place.

Position the splint so that the limb is as comfortable as possible for your patient. After completing the splint, keep an eye on the skin and digits at the end of the limb. If they go numb or turn blue, the splint is too tight and needs to be redone looser.

It should go without saying that any break needs to be checked out and treated by a professional. Besides, how else would you get a cast for everyone to sign?

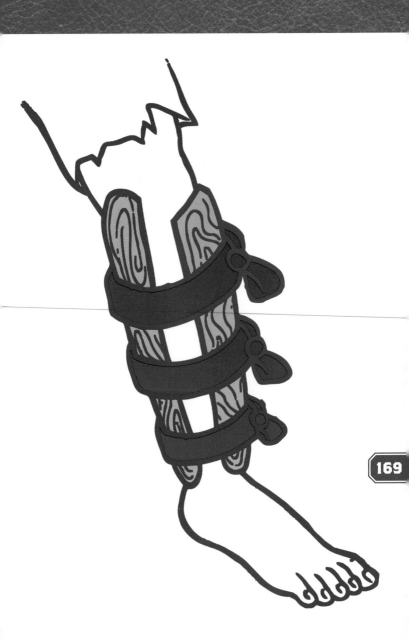

Triage a Gunshot Wound

Gunshot wounds are rare enough that few people outside of an emergency room know how to properly treat one. Be the standout in the crowd when the bullets stop flying, and treat those wounds like nobody's business.

Start by stopping the bleeding. Limiting blood loss is priority one in saving a gunshot victim's life. If the wound or wounds are in the torso, don't elevate the person's legs. Try sealing the wound with plastic or your hand (an increase in air pressure can collapse a lung and complicate the situation). If the victim starts struggling to breathe, remove the wound seal.

Because you have no way of knowing how severe the internal injuries are, the person can quickly fade from a talking, relatively stable condition, to unresponsive unconsciousness. Keep him calm, quiet, and reassured, but don't give him anything to eat or drink.

Fallen victim

He may slip into shock, which will show itself in clammy, cold skin and shallow breathing. Keep a close eye on the situation because it's possible that the person will stop breathing, at which point you should begin CPR. If the person is unconscious but breathing, roll him into the "recovery position" to help keep the airway open. Grab the victim's far leg under the knee and far shoulder, and roll him toward you. He should wind up on his side, with the top hip and knee bent at right angles. Tilt the head back slightly to keep the airway open. Position the person flat on the ground if you need to start CPR.

After preliminary triage, survival hinges on how quickly the victim receives emergency medical care. But don't be tempted to move the victim into your car and race to the emergency room. The wisest thing is to stabilize the victim until the ambulance arrives.

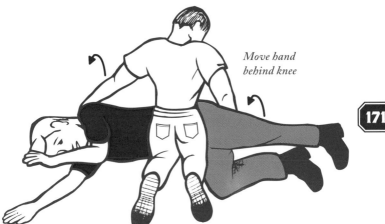

Move hand behind knee

Recovery position

CHAPTER 6

Epicurian Expertise

THE WELL-ROUNDED MAN KNOWS THAT THERE IS SO much more to eating and drinking in style than a cold Bud longneck and a hot Hungry Man dinner. Certainly there's nothing wrong with a good gut-filling meal. But there's nothing wrong with higher-end food and drink. It's not just about being open to experiencing different foods and different spirits—although why wouldn't you be? It's about knowing how you prepare, present and consume that food and drink. It's all a grand ritual.

Mastering the dining arts means letting go of some preconceived notions. No more stuffing your napkin into your shirt collar. You're all grown up and the type of sophisticated dining you'll be doing from time to time requires you keep your napkin in your lap, among many other subtle changes. Start by avoiding reverse snobbery. Sure, it's easy to make fun of dressing for dinner or using multiple forks over the course of one meal. But since when did a Manskills man take the easy way out?

The trick is to understand that dining fine doesn't have to be stuffy. It's not about snooty waiters, uptight blowhard food critics, or drinking to a dollar amount. The real point is that it can be totally fun and cool. You don't have to be a pretentious prat to open a bottle of champagne like a wine captain, or craft an omelet like a chef. Great food and great booze are their own reward and, if you have to dress a bit fancy to get there, you're still the same dude inside.

Moving easily through the vaulted corridors of finer bars and restaurants (or your own culinary wizardry) really only requires a modest amount of knowledge and the skills that let you take advantage of all the pleasure the culinary arts have to offer. Develop a flair for mixing a delicious cocktail, hone your knife-handling abilities for kitchen duty, and perfect your grilling skills, and you will have a food-and-drink repertoire to make any man envious and satisfy everyone's hunger.

Open a Bottle of Champagne

You are not crude. You are a gentleman, who knows that opening a bottle of champagne is one of those subtle, refined skills that are the exact opposite of crude. Subtle being the key word. You will not, in other words, be popping that cork with the sound of a Fourth of July cannon. Nor will you be letting it fly around as a ricochet missile threatening life, limb and property, or at the very least scaring the Hell out of the cat.

No, you have manners. You have style. And you have the good grace to open a bottle of champagne the way a sommelier would. You tear the foil from around the tip of the bottle, exposing the delicate wire cage locked over the cork. Dispose of the foil discreetly. Draping a napkin (preferably cloth) over the top, you unwind the key to that cage, loosening it enough to be removed, but holding it in place just in case the cork decides to suddenly pop without any help—always a possible side effect of the joyous effervescence contained within a bottle of bubbly. In any case, the cork in a bottle of champagne should never be pointed in the direction of another person. Safety and sophistication go hand in hand.

Grip the cork—vis-à-vis the wire cage—tightly, and turn the bottle (not the cork) in one direction until you feel the cork slowly begin to release from the bottle. Rotating the bottle back and forth can break off pieces of cork. Control the release. The cork should come out with a whisper rather than a bang, and all the wine will remain inside, instead of half flowing out in a foaming stream.

Deftly remove the napkin, cage, and cork, and pour a glass of heavenly, fizzing nectar to celebrate your polished presentation skills. Serve in tall flutes to preserve the bubbly goodness.

Decant Fine Wine

If you're going to drop a healthy chunk of a week's pay for that "spectacular" bottle of 40-year-old Cabernet, you should treat it with the respect its age and asking price deserve. Get every bit of flavor out of the wine, without any nasty sediment, by decanting that vintage syrup.

Let the bottle stand upright for an hour or so to ensure that the sediment falls to the bottom. Set up a short taper candle in a candleholder and get your decanter ready. Decanters are essentially chic glass pitchers with long, thin necks and squat, almost-flat bowl-like bodies.

Light the candle. Open the bottle of wine and pick it up. Hold the decanter with the other hand, gripping it by its neck. Now begin pouring wine slowly from the bottle into the decanter, tipping both slightly, so that they form an inverted V. The candle flame should be a couple of inches below the neck of the wine bottle. It's there to shine a critical light through the neck and allow you to see any sediment that might have risen from the bottom. If, at any point in the decanting, you see sediment in the neck, stop and set the wine bottle down. Let the wine settle for another half hour before continuing.

In addition to making sure the wine you serve is sediment-free, the decanting process introduces oxygen as the wine splashes around in the decanter. This releases the flavors and aroma of the wine, making for happy noses and happy tongues at your dinner party table.

Decanting is a must for older wines, but newer wines are filtered as part of their processing, so they don't actually need to be decanted. Even so, decanting a young wine will still release its flavors. Besides, the whole process just looks cool.

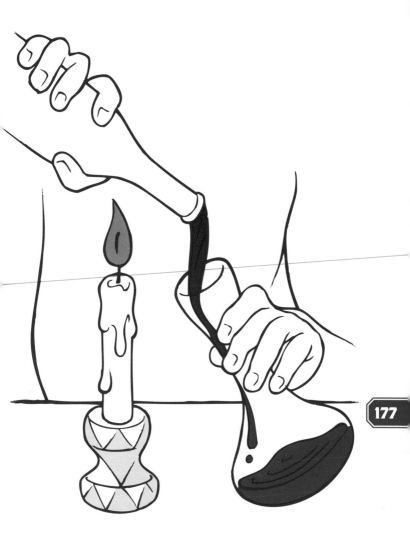

Pop a Beer Without an Opener

You've got the flat screen all warmed up, your special spot on couch ready and waiting, and a half-rack of your favorite microbrews on ice. But those bottles aren't twist-offs and your opener is nowhere to be found. Never fear! All you need is a piece of paper and you'll be good to go. Fold the paper in half, turn it, and fold it in half again. Continue folding it in half in the same direction until it's the width of a stick of gum or thinner. Make each fold crisp by smoothing it down completely. Last, fold the paper in half lengthwise to create a V. Pound the point of the V flat with your fist.

Hold the beer with your fingers around the neck and the web between thumb and index finger pressing down on the cap edge opposite where you'll pop it (this provides leverage). Wedge the opener in between the top of your index finger where it curves around the neck and the underside of the cap's lip. In one smooth movement, lever the opener up, keeping your index finger tight as the lever point, and exerting downward pressure on the skin web covering the far edge of the cap. With some practice, you'll be able to do it consistently. The opener, however, will only hold up for one beer.

But wait. What if you're out at the lake with a bunch of your beer-drinking peeps and nobody brought an opener or a piece of paper? Pull out your keys and use the ragged, tooth side of one as a pry to bend the edges of the cap out one section at a time. Work halfway around the cap and it should pop off without any trouble. Just make sure your keys find their way to the designated driver.

Master the Martini

Nothing can put a man in a James Bond mood quite like fixing his best steely stare over the elegant rim of a martini glass. And to hold a martini glass, one should be drinking a martini. It follows that, if you're going to drink the things, you should know exactly how to craft the perfect version.

A true martini is made with gin, the best money can buy. You can use vodka if you must, but you aren't a purist and you'll offend those who are. Gin, sir, is the preferred liquor of all double-Os, and those who would call themselves double-Os. And for a true classic martini, grab yourself a bottle of London dry gin (that dark green one or the light blue one or the one with the funny looking palace guard on the label all will do nicely, to name a few). Avoid the fancy, boutique gins that have notes of raspberry and other decidedly non-martini flavors.

Elegance is so often a matter of simplicity, and no more so than with the martini. It is both the most elegant and stylish cocktail, and the simplest. Only two ingredients in the whole thing. Combine four parts of the best gin available with 1 part vermouth. Mix these briskly in a shaker of ice—just long enough to chill the liquid, but not so long as to pollute it with water. (Shaken or stirred doesn't really make a difference.) Pour the resulting elixir into the classic stemmed martini glass and drop in an olive.

Martini in hand, you are now sufficiently well equipped to pull off a rousing round of baccarat, romance that lovely who has captured your heart as well as your eye, and even drop the witty bon mot. However, do stay away from high-speed boat chases and hand-to-combat. You might spill.

Ace a Wine Tasting

At one point or another, the woman of your dreams is going to want to go on a mini-vacation to wine country. You'll visit a slew of wineries and try a bunch of wines. This is your chance to present yourself as a worldly gentlemen, cultured and sure of your palate.

The wine-tasting ritual follows some basic guidelines. Get into the process, and you may even find it enjoyable. Always suppress the urge to gulp.

Someone will pour you a smidgen of wine. Swirl the wine around the bowl of the glass to introduce oxygen and release the aroma. Taste being mostly smell, a good sniff will tell you a lot about a wine.

Next, look at the wine. Watch how it washes down the glass and note its viscosity or thickness. Thicker wines are often more alcoholic and more full-bodied. Experts say these wines have legs. Study the color with the wine backlit. Older reds tend toward a brownish color, while older whites yellow with age. Deeper colors often connote a richer, more complex wine. Got it? Good.

Draw a small sip of the wine into your mouth and roll it around. Don't make faces and don't swallow. The idea is to discover all the flavors of the wine, as well as the general texture. Don't be surprised if you aren't noticing the "traces of pepper and blueberry" everybody else is yammering about. Just nod and look contemplative.

The winery will have supplied spit buckets, but nobody's going to look sideways if you swallow. Just be aware that tasting a couple dozen wines a sip at a time can lead to some time in buzzville.

Everyone will discuss the wine, so pick one thing you noticed about the color and the flavor. Stay away from references to Boone's Farm and you'll do fine.

Pour a Black and Tan

No offense to the Queen, but England has never really been known for its cuisine. Bangers and mash, beef-and-kidney pie, and bubble and squeak don't draw much fondness outside the borders of the Union Jack. But when it comes to manly beers and manly beer drinking, ah, that's a different story.

The Brits are to thank for the tastiest beer "cocktail", called a black and tan. It's a classic mix of pale ale or lager and dark beer, such as a stout or porter. Knowing how to mix one is essential if you're to be called the king among your mates.

Use a clean, refrigerated, pint glass and pull it out only when you're ready to pour the drink. Use a pouring spoon, which you can buy from a specialty shop, or bend your own from a cheap piece of flatware. The spoon is bent nearly into an L, downward from the underside of the bowl.

Now pour your favorite pale ale (Harp is traditional) until the glass is half full. Hold the spoon with the bottom of the bowl facing up and tilted slightly. Slowly pour Guinness down over the bowl of the spoon. If it splashes, you're pouring too fast. Pour steadily, and don't worry if the two beers seem to be mixing. Once you've filled the glass, let the drink settle, and a clear separation will be apparent. The denser pale ale sinks to the bottom, while the airier structure of the Guinness allows it to float in a separate layer on top.

It's a lovely drink to look at, but even lovelier to quaff. After a couple, you begin to see just how those people across the pond manage to throw down "cullen skink" and blood pudding. The right amount of black and tan can make anyone beautiful and anything tasty.

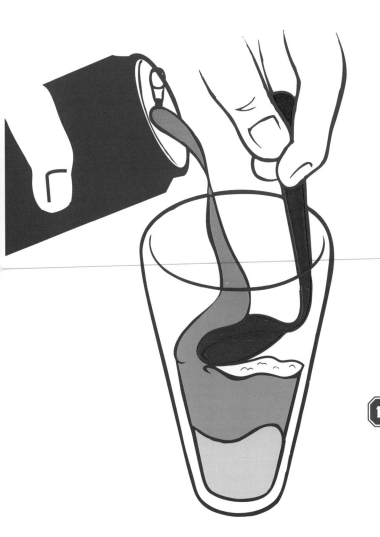

Do a Shot

Throwing back a shot is much more than simply having a drink; it is, in fact, a time-honored tradition, one that draws men together in celebration. Celebration of what is not always clear, but that's not important. What is important is that the ritual be performed correctly.

So, rule one: If you suggest the shot, you now own the ritual. Decide on the type of shot. Real men do real shots, which means bourbon, whiskey, vodka, and, if you're within a thousand miles of the equator, rum. Mixed shots of kamikazes are for lunkheads who don't know better, and bachelorette parties. Scotch, at least decent scotch, is sipped and therefore not suitable for shooting. Schnapps and Jagermeister are for ski outings only.

Rule two: Doing a shot means honoring something or somebody. As the shot caller, you make the toast. It can be short and sweet (the best toasts always are), but it should thoughtful, witty, or both. Gather your partners in crime and make your toast. Clink glasses, then down the poison in one gulp. The trick is to open your throat and convince yourself that you are simply tossing back water.

Rule three: Understand that if you refuse to do a shot for any reason short of alcoholism, you will be thought of as a lesser man in perpetuity. The same is true if you don't finish the shot in one go, although that's certainly better than refusing it outright.

Also be ready for repercussions. It's only gentlemanly to buy a shot for someone who has bought a shot for you. If you bought several friends a shot, they will each, in their turn reciprocate. All of which can turn a pleasant evening of camaraderie into a short blur and a long hangover. But all in all, a shot well done.

Mix the Perfect Margarita

When the hot weather hits, you only need one swimming pool, one pair of trunks, one really good beach tunes CD, one bottle of sunscreen, and one pair of hip shades. Oh, and one incredibly refreshing, wonderfully intoxicating, stupendously sweetly sour cocktail. That cocktail is the margarita. Blending the perfect one is a way to make sure you're the one man everybody absolutely has to have at their summer party.

When you think of a margarita, chances are that you're picturing a blender drink, possibly pink or red, that's made with crushed ice. Well, that kind of margarita is for TexMex restaurant chains and bachelorette parties. A real margarita is mixed straight up and served over ice cubes, just like Old Montezuma meant it to be.

A great—truly great—margarita starts with the ingredients. Use a top-shelf, aged, agave tequila; lesser quality (cheaper) tequilas not only bring down the flavor potential, they add to the hangover potential. Use Cointreau, not triple sec. Fresh lime juice only. And that's all you'll need. The secret is in how you mix them.

Fill a shaker half full of ice and add three parts tequila, two parts fresh squeezed lime juice, and two parts Cointreau. Stir or shake vigorously.

Prepare the glass by rubbing a lime around its rim, and dipping the rim in a saucer of coarse salt, like you would for a tequila shot. Fill the glass with ice (cubes, or crushed if you prefer, but cubes are manlier) and pour the mix into the glass. Garnish with a slice of lime, and make it a whole, silver-dollar shaped slice with a little cut to fit over the rim: you don't want to skimp on the citrus. Now prepare to make many, many more of these fiesta favorites. For the moment you are the Man, and the Man must keep pouring. Cue the mariachis.

Drink Absinthe

The drinking man should be a daring man. And only a daring man will plunge into the ritual and myth of that jaded spirit known as the Green Fairy, absinthe. This drink first gained fame—actually infamy—in the late 1800s, in France. The liquor is a distinct emerald green, accounting for the nickname (okay, so ignore the nickname). Featuring a bitter, licorice flavor, absinthe is brewed from a variety of herbs including wormwood, which is thought to be responsible for the drink's more heady qualities. Absinthe is a strong cocktail, as much as 70 percent alcohol. It has long been associated with bohemianism and debauchery, and is often credited with drug-like effects, including hallucinations and psychotic episodes. Still up for a sip, big man?

Take some comfort that its rumored psychoactive properties have never been clinically proven. Then dive into the ritual that fueled famous French philosophers to new heights of creativity.

To create the drink as those brave souls did, you'll need a perforated spoon (flat absinthe spoons are available in specialty shops, but you can use a slotted spoon), a cube of sugar and 3 to 5 ounces of pure, chilled spring water.

Pour a shot of absinthe in a tall stem glass. Hold the spoon over the glass with the cube of sugar in the center of the spoon. Now slowly drip the water over the sugar, dissolving it into the glass. The sugar softens the bitterness and the water cuts the kick. The sugar water also changes the color of the drink from clear green, to an opaque, milky hue. When the sugar is all dissolved, sip the drink and wait for the visions to arrive. After all, you too, may be full of philosophy just waiting to pour out.

Select the Best Steak

All the grilling skill in the world amounts to nothing if the meat you cook isn't up to snuff. That's why knowing how to choose a good piece of meat is every bit as important as knowing how to cook it.

First off, you need to look for the right cut. The most popular cuts for grilling are loin cuts, which include the T-bone, tenderloin, porterhouse, sirloin, top sirloin, and New York strip. All are cut from parts of the cow that see little use when the animal is alive, and are therefore more tender. Flank steaks and other cuts from more muscular tissue are also good for grilling, but because they fight back a little more when you chew them you don't normally serve them up at a steak fry. Slice them up for fajitas or a steak salad, though, and your guests will swoon from all the flavor.

Along with the cut, pay attention to the grade: prime, choice, or select. Provided by the USDA, the grade reflects the age of the animal and the uniformity of the marbling (fat streaks) in the meat. Prime is rare, expensive and usually gobbled up by high-end restaurants, but if you spot some jump on it: you won't be disappointed. Choice is great for home grilling. Select can be used, but you must shop carefully.

The best grilling steaks will be found in a butcher's case, not on a foam plate and wrapped in plastic. The meat should be firm to the touch, with a uniform, fine texture and a bright cherry red color. Avoid meat that is deep, dark red, or has any areas of gray. You also want to look for even marbling throughout the meat, but without large sections of fat on the outside. The fat itself should be slightly off-white, but not yellow or gray.

Grill the Perfect Steak

Lord of the cookout. Now that's a title you can carry proudly. But if you're going to rule the back deck Weber like real royalty, you must first know how to take an ideal cut of meat and turn it into the juiciest, tastiest, tenderest steak that ever found its way onto a plate.

Begin with the best meat you can find—ideally dry aged New York strip. Then prepare the grilling surface. You want at least two zones ready to go in the grill—high heat and medium heat. On a gas grill, this will be fairly easy to achieve. If you're charcoal grilling, you'll mound the charcoal to two different heights.

Sear the steak on both sides, until you see the characteristic crosshatched sear marks, moving the steak with tongs (never use a fork—puncturing a steak releases the juices you just seared the steak to hold in). Now move the steak to the medium heat side, and cook to your preferred state of doneness.

You can tell how done a steak is by feel. If you poke the steak and it is very soft, it's rare. If it gives just a little, it's medium rare. Firm with slight give means medium, and hard means well done (which, if you are paying attention at all, you'll never experience).

You can use a basic hand test to determine doneness. The fleshy pad beneath your thumb acts as a poke gauge. Touch the thumb to the index finger and touch the pad; that's rare. Thumb and middle finger is medium rare; thumb and ring finger is medium; and pinkie is medium well. When the steak is cooked the way you like it, pull it off the grill, let it rest for 4 or 5 minutes, top with a pat of butter and serve.

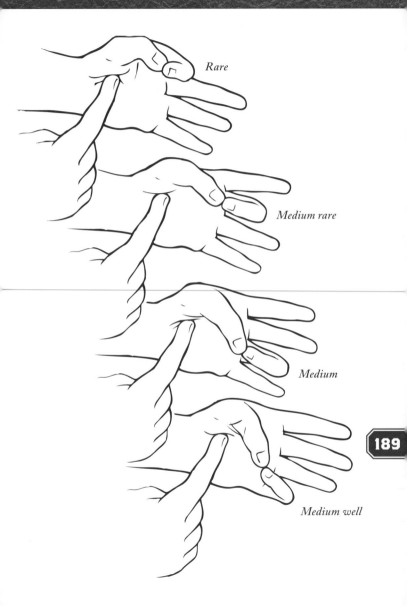

Rare

Medium rare

Medium

Medium well

Season Cast Iron

Let's talk cookware for a moment big fella. Rule one: Leave the non-stick aluminum pots and pans for someone else. The original, best, and man-cookingest cookware is pure cast iron. Forged from fire as hot as the center of the Earth (okay, maybe not, but really, really hot), cast iron makes an ideal cooking surface. It is an incredibly consistent conductor of heat and cast-iron pots and pans don't have hot spots. It allows you to control the cooking temperature precisely, and if seasoned and cared for correctly cast iron becomes virtually nonstick. Plus, a cast iron skillet is an awesome weapon to use on a home intruder. And, perhaps best of all, you can buy cast iron cookware at sporting goods stores and even at some hardware stores: talk about your Manskillets!

A new cast iron pan must be seasoned before it's used. You've seen what rookies do to your Fantasy Football rankings, so you know how valuable a little seasoning can be. Seasoning is a process that seals microscopic pores and pits in the metal. First, rub a light coat of vegetable oil onto the cooking surface. The surface should look dry when you finish. Next, bake the pan upside-down in an oven set to 500°F for about 45 minutes. Let the pan cool to room temperature and you've seasoned it.

Seasoning is actually an ongoing process. Each time you cook, you lay down a layer of oil or grease. But you'll ruin the seasoning if you let food sit in the pot or pan or clean it in the wrong way. Clean up cast-iron cookware as soon as you're done cooking, washing it lightly with warm water and a little dish soap. Dry the pot or pan thoroughly before putting it away. Never put cast iron in a dishwasher, unless you're really fond of eating rust.

Care for Copper

Once you reach a certain level of cooking expertise you're going to want high-performance tools to help you take your game to the next level. Along with a selection of cast iron skillets (previous page), that means copper pots and pans. Copper is a spectacular conductor of heat, and gives you maximum control over cooking temperature. Copper pans are also lightweight, which makes them easy to handle. Although you can't sear foods the same way in copper as you can with cast-iron cookware, copper is a superior material for fine sauces and other complex recipes. Most copper cookware, like the very popular Revereware, are copper only where they contact the heat source and are lined with stainless steel.

Copper cookware is also beautiful. That's why so many hardcore home cooks display their copper pieces by hanging them from pot racks.

Keeping your copper pots and pans looking and cooking their best is a matter of attention to detail and a little maintenance. Allow your copper pieces to cool completely before washing. Wash them in hot soapy water with a non-abrasive scrubbing pad. Copper cookware should never air dry; dry your pots and pans with a clean, soft towel immediately after washing.

You will, inevitably, deal with tarnish or verdigris (a green coating produced by a chemical reaction as copper ages) marring the look of your copper ware. You'll find a number of commercial cleaners available, but none works better than a simple homemade paste of lemon juice, flour and salt mixed together. Rub the paste over the entire copper surface, using a soft cloth. When you're finished, rinse with warm water and dry with a clean towel. The chemical reaction does all the cleaning for you. And remember: like cast iron, copper cookware should never be put in a dishwasher.

Cook Fish over an Open Fire

Caught or bought, fish cooked over an open flame is the best kind. Hone your skill so that the fish is perfectly firm and flaky when you pull it off the fire, and you'll be able to whip out a delicious dinner over the campfire or on the backyard barbecue.

Whether you grill steaks or filets, you want thick cuts to throw on the flame. This lessens the chance of messy breakage when you turn the fish. Look for an even-width cut, so that a thinner portion doesn't overcook.

Cover the fish in a thin coat of olive oil (it shouldn't drip off) before cooking. This ensures the fish doesn't stick to the grill while adding some mouthwatering flavor. Preheat the fire and drop the fish on the grill. If you want those great looking crosshatch sear marks, give the fish a quarter turn after a few minutes.

Flip the fish only once, when the edges are opaque and flaky. You'll know the whole cut is done when it's completely flaky and opaque through and through. Any juice running out will be clear.

Go a little bit more rustic by impaling a whole fish on a spit, and turning it over an open fire. Once it's done, you'll be able to peel off the crispy skin, and flake the meat off the bones. (This works best for saltwater fish, which have larger bones).

For a campfire feast, create a cooking pouch from a large tin foil sheet. Oil up a couple filets, and place them in the pouch with a chopped bulb of wild garlic, a pinch of salt and pepper, and ½ cup of beer. Seal the pouch and drop it on the coals. After about 12 minutes, you'll have some of the juiciest, most delectable fish you've ever chomped on.

Grill Corn on the Cob

Just about any dinner food can be grilled. And one of the best is corn on the cob. You've already got the grill fired up, so what sense does it make to run back in the house and boil your corn?

The two ways to grill corn on the cob are in the husk or in aluminum foil. It's your call, because the corn is going to taste the same either way.

Go natural by peeling the outer layer, leaving most of the husk intact. Twist the remaining husk to break it open slightly. Soak the cobs in a pot of cold water for 15 minutes. Completely cover the ears with water.

Preheat the grill to medium while the corn soaks. When the corn is ready, remove the silk and squeeze the husks back down over the corn. Close the tops with twine or string.

Grill the corn by rotating as they cook to keep them from burning on one side. Once you've turned the ears completely around, place them off to the side and close the cover. Grill for about 15 minutes more. When the husks darken and pull away from the tip of the cob, pull the ears off the grill. Remove them with tongs, and peel using an oven mitt or towel. Brush off any ash or residue on the corn, and serve with butter.

To cook the ears in foil, remove the husks and silk entirely. Soak the corn in cold water for 10 minutes, and roll them tightly in large sheets of foil, twisting the ends shut. Grill for fifteen minutes, turning the ears every couple of minutes. When fully grilled, individual kernels will squirt liquid when squeezed. Use an oven mitt to remove the foil and serve as before, with plenty of butter.

Carve the Bird

They sit you at the head of the table for a reason, and it ain't because you're easy on the eyes. Someone needs to carve that beautifully tanned bird. And you are on the hot seat.

Cutting up a roasted turkey or chicken isn't open-heart surgery. With a sure hand, the right knife, and a step-by-step process, you'll be serving bird slices in no time.

Equipping yourself with the right tool for the job will make the carving go much easier. Don't use an electric knife. It doesn't allow enough control and you're likely to shred the bird rather than carve it. A sharp, quality 10-inch carving knife is ideal.

The turkey or chicken should rest for about 10 minutes after you take it out of the oven and before you start cutting, to allow the juices to settle and saturate the meat. When you're ready to start the feast, take your weapon in hand and go to work. Remove the legs one at a time, by holding the leg firmly and sliding the knife into the crease between thigh and body. Slice down until you come to the joint, and pull the leg off. Put the legs on the serving platter. Sever drumstick from thigh if you want, or not if you prefer.

Remove each wing by forking it and cutting horizontally above the wing joint. Slice down from that cut and remove the wing.

Now start the real carving. Slice halfway up the breast, cutting vertically until you come even with the wing joint horizontal cut. This first slice should fall right off the bird. Continue cutting slices off the breast (thinner, evenly cut slices are a sign of knife mastery), working your way up to the crest. Cut the other side, and present the platter of your skillful slashings to your hungry fans.

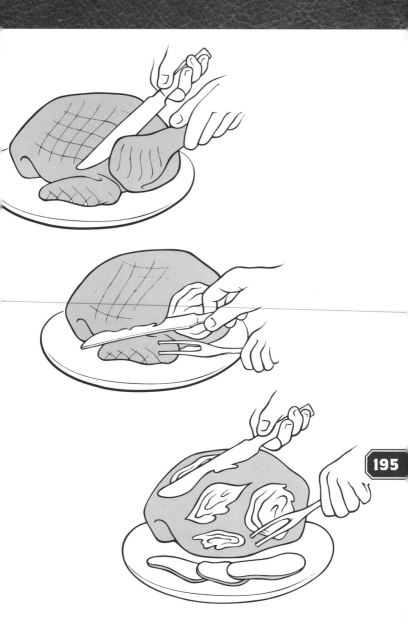

Cook a Lobster

You could do a lot worse for a perfect meal than a whole lobster. That sweet white meat is the stuff of heavenly kitchen dreams, and it's an easy delicacy to prepare.

Fill a large stockpot about ¾ full of cold water. Add 2 tablespoons sea salt for every quart of water. There should be enough water to cover the lobster. You can add white wine or spices to the water, but these add little if anything to the flavor of the meat.

Heat until the water is at a roiling boil (really boiling = roiling). Grab your prey around the body, just behind the claws, and remove the rubber bands (if there are any) from his claws. It's okay if you need to use tongs.

Those claws will move around even though he can't possibly reach backwards. Drop the thing into the pot and slam the lid down on top.

Generally speaking, you'll need about 10 to 12 minutes to cook a one-pound lobster. Add 2 minutes for each additional half-pound. This timing may vary slightly, so check your crustacean periodically. He's done when he is bright red and an antenna can be pulled off without resistance. You can also check by pulling off a small side leg. If the meat is white and firm, he's ready for the dinner table.

Serve lobster with the traditional drawn butter (melted butter that has been strained of solids) or less traditional mayonnaise. Lemon slices are excellent accompaniment as well.

Use lobster crackers (special pliers-like utensils) to crack the shell, and small forks to get at that lovely meat. Most of the meat is in the tail and claws. Avoid the yellowish green tomally, the sac right behind the eyes, and the dark vein that runs up the tail.

Boil a Perfect Egg

Consider the hard-boiled egg. A perfect use of the hen's fruit, a handy snack in its own protective case, ready to eat with just a sprinkle of salt. It's a protein-packed quick breakfast, a mini-meal on the go, a simple and wonderful product of the kitchen requiring little in the way preparation or fuss.

Simple as it is though, it's also easy to screw up.

Oddly, overcooking is more often the problem than undercooking. You'll know an overcooked hardboiled egg by its signature greenish ring around a greenish or gray yolk. Overdone hardboiled eggs also taste slightly of sulfur. Only the devil finds that taste pleasant.

For perfect hardboiled eggs start with eggs that have sat in the refrigerator for 3 days or more. Older eggs will be easier to peel. Put the eggs in a saucepan, covering them with cold water to at a least an inch above the eggs. Now turn on the heat and bring those babies to a boil.

Once the water is at a rolling boil, turn off the heat, cover the eggs, and let them sit for 10 minutes. After the time has elapsed, drain the water out of the pan, and start running cold water over the eggs. Leave the water running until the eggs are cold.

Refrigerate the eggs in a closed container (the smell can get into other food) until you're ready to eat them. The shells should crack open and peel easily after a sharp rap on the counter. If the shells are little difficult to peel, roll the egg between your palm and a hard surface while pressing down firmly with your palm. That will break the shell into lots of small sections, which can easily be shed under running water. There you have it, your own little power snack.

Make the Perfect Omelet

Man does not live by donuts alone. No, on occasion, a man must start his day with a healthy, filling, and tasty breakfast. He must turn to eggs. You can scramble them, but if you want to make eggs an all-in-one meal, make an omelet. Omelets are actually easy and quick to make, and a filling breakfast.

Use two large eggs. A two-egg omelet is easier to handle and will easily satisfy even a man-size hunger. Crack the eggs by rapping them on a flat, hard surface. Pop the shells open along the cracks you've made, and drop the eggs into a bowl. Add two tablespoons of water and beat thoroughly.

Assemble the ingredients for your fillings—cheese, bell peppers, whatever (the classic French omelet has no fillings). If you are adding veggies, like peppers or onions, sauté them first—they can't possibly cook in the short time they'll be on the burner with the eggs. Heat an omelet pan on high until it's really hot. Drop a pad of butter into the center of the pan and swirl it around.

When the butter is melted and has just started to brown, pour the eggs into the pan. Use a spatula to pull the edges in toward the center at different points around the pan, allowing the uncooked egg on top to run out and fill those areas. Soon, you'll have very little uncooked egg left.

Now spread the filling over one half of the eggs (the side opposite your dominant hand—for ease of flipping). Use your spatula to pry up the edge of the other side, and flip it over on top of the fillings. Let it cook for a few seconds more and then, aided by the spatula, slide your delectable creation out onto a plate. If you accidentally turn less than half the omelet, flip the filled side that same amount, to make an "envelope" omelet.

Sauté Like a Chef

Sautéing is to cooking what power nailing is to home repair: the coolest, manliest technique you can use. The technique gets it name from the French word meaning "to jump," because the food is meant to be moved quickly. Sautéing involves pan cooking any kind of food quickly, using oil or butter to rapidly transfer heat from the source to the food. Sauté just about anything, from small medallions of beef, to a panful of vegetables. The only limitation is that all the food should be roughly the same size.

Use a pan with sloped slides and large enough to hold what you want to cook. Preheat the pan over a burner set on medium. Toss in some butter or oil. Butter is used more often, because it lends a richer flavor to the food. But oil is generally used at higher temperatures—anything above 375°F—at which butter would burn and smoke rather then melt. Oil can also be used for a healthier meal, and some cooks prefer to use a mix of oil and butter. Experiment to find what works best for you.

Whichever lubricant you use, allow a moment for it to get hot before tossing in the food. Butter should melt, stop foaming and begin to brown. Then put whatever you're cooking into the pan. Cook meat and fish to the doneness you would choose when grilling. Cook vegetables until you can easily slice through them with the edge of a spatula.

Depending on what spices you use and how sticky the food is (and whether you plan on making a sauce from the leavings), you can deglaze the pan right before removing the food. To do this, splash a bit of alcohol such as cooking sherry into the pan, and allow the flame from the burner to ignite it.

Whip up Perfect Pasta

No man really ever has to know how to make a chocolate soufflé, but every man worth his salt absolutely must know how to rustle up a big serving of perfect pasta.

That means noodles that don't stick together, aren't mushy, and hold sauce like they were married to it. That perfection begins with the water, and you need lots of it: 4 to 5 quarts for any amount over half a pound of pasta. Abundant water makes it easier to get long, skinny pasta into the water quicker, makes for a quicker return to boiling after the pasta has been tossed in, and washes away more of the starch that contributes to sticking.

Bring the water to a rolling boil before you add the pasta. Salt the water after it starts boiling—1 tablespoon will do it. Then stir every couple of minutes to maintain a separation between the noodles.

Check the pasta often to see if it's done. There's only one way to do that, and that's with your teeth. Pluck a noodle out of the pot, rinse it in cold water so that you don't burn your tongue, and bite it. Pasta is done when it's "al dente" or "to the teeth." Meaning, it isn't crunchy, but still provides a little resistance.

When your pasta is done, drain it in a colander. Don't you dare rinse those noodles with cold water. Yes, your mother did that, but then again, she considered Velveeta the all-purpose cheese, right?

Instead, immediately after the pasta is completely drained, pop it back in the pot or in a bowl, and toss it with a ladle full of sauce. The noodles will absorb the sauce's flavors and the sauce will help prevent any sticking between the noodles. Serve right away, for some serious cases of happy stomach.

Make a Display Garnish

A well-cooked meal is incomplete without garnish. Given how easy they are to create, there's just no reason not to garnish. Just about any small, colorful food item can be made into a garnish. If you're rushed or unsure of your fine motor skills, stick to the simple ones.

A rose is a nice finishing touch for a chicken or fish dish. Peel tomato skin with a potato peeler, keeping the peel an even width. Pinch the end of the peel and wind it tightly into an open coil and voila, a rose.

A strawberry fan is a great dessert ornament. Make a series of thin, parallel cuts across the face of the strawberry, from just below the stem side, through the tip side. Hold the stem and press down on the strawberry to fan out the slices and create a delicious dessert garnish.

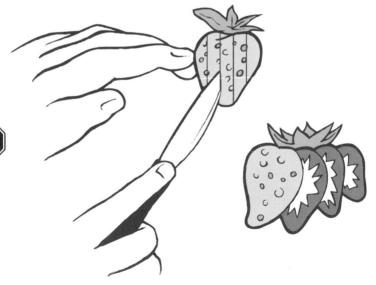

Taste Cheese Like a Cheese Taster

If your idea of enjoying cheese is slapping a slice of Velveeta on a Ritz, it's definitely time to up your game. You don't want to be stuck looking like Jethro Bodine when you find yourself in the middle of an actual cheese tasting (especially if it was that special someone's idea), which means mastering the basics of the process. Simple as the subject may seem, keep an open mind: the vast number of cheese types and variables in the aging process make cheese tasting every bit as complex as wine tasting.

Cheese releases its bouquet most fully when it's warm, so cheese for a tasting should be at room temperature. Slice into the cheese, taking a sample from as close to the center as possible. Edges exposed to air or plastic wrap form a thin protective skin that masks flavors and aromas. To keep from overwhelming your senses, start with the mildest cheese on the platter and work up to the strongest, and always taste an appropriately small sample.

Because taste is actually largely a product of smell, you'll want to start by grabbing a big whiff of the cheese you just cut (oh grow up). Concentrate on the smell and you should be able to detect and separate out several undertones, such as grass (the main cow food), citrus, or butter, and more general qualities such as sharpness. Take a bite of the cheese and work it along your tongue from front to back, exhaling through your nose (that will invigorate the olfactory receptors). Press the cheese up against the roof of your mouth. You should now be able to comment knowingly about the texture and density, how intense the taste is, and other qualities such as saltiness and specific flavors. Just be careful never to use the phrase, "Reminiscent of a fine Velveeta."

Sharpen a Knife

It's the poor craftsman that blames his tools, but that's just more reason for the craftsman to care for his tools. You wouldn't leave your circular saw out in the rain, and you shouldn't let your prep knife get so dull that it tears what it's supposed to cut.

Avoid dollar-store sharpeners. A cheap sharpener is as likely to damage the edge as it is to sharpen it. And don't just turn to the rod-like steel that comes with most kitchen knife sets; that's only meant to tune up the edge between sharpenings.

Instead, get yourself a bench, or sharpening, stone.

The stone has a coarse and fine side that are used in tandem to produce a super sharp knife edge. Coat the stone with lubricant meant for the type you're using. A water stone is soaked in water. Most other stones use mineral or machine oil.

Start on the coarse side and hold the knife edge away from you and down at an angle to the stone (about 20 degrees for most knives, and 10 degrees for Japanese knives or filet knives). Keep your wrists stiff and slide the knife along the face of the stone, sweeping it sideways as you go to sharpen the entire blade. Flip the knife when the first side is sharp, and repeat the process on the other side, until you've built up a burr on the edge. Now do the same using the fine side of the stone. Stop when the knife can cleanly slice through a piece of paper held up on edge.

Finish up by honing the knife with a steel. It will remove any microscope burr and align the edge perfectly. Slide each side of the knife along the steel, holding the knife at a slightly greater angle than you used on the stone.

Pick the Perfect Cigar

There's no better way to celebrate those memorable manly occasions—the end of bachelorhood, a birthday ending in 0—than with an equally memorable smoke. Anywhere scotch or bourbon are to be served, they can only be made better with the right cigar.

Finding a firestick that will live up to the occasion is a matter of knowing what makes a fine cigar. The best way is to leisurely inspect several in the comfort of your local cigar shop (an essential part of any cigar-smoking experience). Start by choosing a size.

The length of the cigar increases smoking time. Inexperienced smokers are generally wiser to start out with a shorter cigar—something around 5 inches. This will moderate the time spent in what might be an overwhelming experience.

The other measure is the "ring" or diameter (measured with ring gauges in increments of 1/60th of an inch). Larger ring cigars are usually better cigars—smoother to smoke, and burn more evenly and slowly. It's reasonable to start out with a ring of 44 to 48.

Once you've chosen a size, inspect potential candidates. Don't roll the cigar between your fingers because you could damage the outer layer of tobacco, known as the wrapper. (If you don't buy it, you're doing a disservice to the customer who does). Just hold it lightly between your fingers and feel the body. The cigar should not be overly soft, nor should there be lumps or specific soft spots anywhere along its length.

The color of the wrapper (the outer layer of tobacco) will tell a lot about the cigar. The wrapper should be evenly colored with no discernible blotches, and without any sign of loosening or cracking. The exposed end should not have variations in color, because noticeable differences can indicate an inferior leaf and improper rolling. Both will make the cigar burn unevenly and taste odd.

The actual color of the wrapper indicates the cigar's flavor. The darker the wrapper, the sweeter the cigar will likely be, and the more full-bodied. Cigar colors range widely from the light brown sugar hue of Claro, to the almost ebony Oscuro.

Generally though, if you stay away from the cheapest cigars and those that display obvious signs of defect, you'll have a pleasant smoking experience. Inferior or damaged cigars may show themselves in cracked wrappers, a whitish mold, blotchy appearances, or tiny holes in the wrapper that indicate the tobacco was attacked by a tobacco beetle.

Be ready to drop a pretty dime on the smoke of choice, and don't hesitate to ask the guy behind the counter; chances are he's a smoker himself and can lead you to the choice best suited for your experience and tastes.

Enjoy a Fine Smoke

When you've dropped a healthy chunk of change on an excellent cigar, it only makes sense to follow the established ritual of how to smoke it. You want to get every puff of enjoyment out of that cigar. To do that, focus on covering the four bases: Cutting, lighting, smoking, and finishing. Each can be done in a right and wrong way. The right way not only makes the whole smoke more enjoyable, it makes you look like the worldly chap you are.

Cutting a cigar is a much misunderstood and incorrectly executed maneuver. The idea is to cut off the "cap" of the cigar—the small, circular twist of tobacco at the end that will go into your mouth—to create a perfect opening for smoking. Don't cut too far into the cigar or you lose precious tobacco. The cigar is best cut with a single-blade guillotine cutter. The sharp blade slices cleanly down through the cigar right where the cap connects to the body, leaving a flat front. Two-bladed bypass cutters are a second choice. But this is for certain: never bite the tip off a cigar. It's a move right out of vintage movies, and that's where it should stay. In addition to pulling pieces of tobacco off your tongue for minutes afterward, you'll likely degrade the structure of the cigar.

Now light your smoke. But don't use just any flame source. A butane cigar lighter or special long cigar matches are ideal. Regular matches can impart an ammonia or sulfur smell that will be inhaled through the cigar, while regular cigarette lighters carry a fuel smell. The cigar should be lit by drawing in several shallow puffs while rotating the end through the flame, with the cigar held at a slight angle (about 45 degrees) to the flame. Light the end evenly and, when the cigar is fully lit, blow gently on the end.

Now comes the best part. Take the smoke into your mouth with a strong draw, but don't inhale. Allow it to swirl around, hitting the full breadth of your palette and savoring the flavor. Slowly blow out the smoke.

After about 10 puffs, remove the cigar band. This lets the cigar warm up so that the band's glue softens, and allows it to be removed without damaging the cigar's wrapper.

The cigar is finished when you decide you've tasted the best part of it. Most cigars become stronger, more bitter, and burn hotter the more they burn down. When you've had enough, sit the cigar in an ashtray and let it burn out of its own accord. Stubbing a cigar out can make for an unpleasant aroma throughout the room.

CHAPTER 7

Romantic Prowess

INSIDE THE GRUFF, TOUGH, MUSCULAR EXTERIOR OF
a skillful man beats the heart of an incurable romantic. Yes, it's true. Part of
being the complete package is knowing the art of the mythic Don Juan, that
singular ability to make the right woman happy for a long, long time. The truly
accomplished Manskills man is just like really good candy—hard and crunchy
on the outside, soft and gooey on the inside.

That's okay, because he knows that handling himself with grace and style
means managing relationships with the opposite sex. Never uncomplicated,
those relationships. Whether they be with a wife, girlfriend, or potential
girlfriend, those relationships inevitably involve a spider's web of friends,
family, issues and, yes, feelings. (Don't make that face.) But you can hold
your own in a fight, fix just about anything that might break, and pull off a
high-society dinner.

There will be parents to meet and win over, and they will be critical. There will
be flirting to be completed, and snippy friends to be convinced. And, of course,
there will be sensitive listening to be done. That's a lot to handle with football
season fast approaching, but you're up to it. The reward is, one day at the end
of that relationship rainbow, a proposal will be made for a life spent forever
together. Hello, Hallmark?

Yes, any Manskills dude is much more comfortable under the hood of his car
or even fighting large, angry beasts in the wild. Those are built into your nature,
part of your Y chromosome. But the true man will not shy from the task at
hand; he will rise to the challenge of romance. He will do everything necessary
to woo. Nothing intimidates him and, truth be told, he has feelings. No, he
doesn't cry at Kodak commercials, and he doesn't hunker down for a week at a
time with a pint of ice cream and daytime TV when things go wrong. But he
does have feelings.

Let's remember though, mum's the word.

Impress Her with Chivalry

Hey, we're all trying to answer that greatest of great questions: What do women really want? Access to the remote? Bad boy or good guy? You may never know everything your woman wants, but this is guaranteed: she will always appreciate chivalry.

Chivalry is thoughtfulness and manners by any other name. It is a million small ways of letting her know she matters to you. Extended to the larger group of women in the world, chivalry shows that you are a man of polish and class.

Opening the door for a woman is the height of chivalry, and an increasingly lost art. It is a simple gesture of respect and courtesy and, for something that takes seconds, it can make a permanent impression.

Nowhere is chivalry more impressive than in social events. Pull out her chair when you arrive at the table. Rise when she—or any woman—leaves the table, and when she returns. Women order first and are served first, and if the wait staff don't know that, discreetly steer the service in that direction.

The simple graciousness of chivalry extends beyond the formal. Offer her your hand when she's getting out of the car, or climbing steep steps in high heels. Put your hand on the small of her back and lead you both through the crowd with your shoulder forward so that the crowd does not press in on her. She always enters a room first.

Chivalry also serves in private. A spontaneous compliment with no hidden agenda is a small present you give to a woman. It has to be sincere and subtle. Likewise, sacrifice your jacket if she doesn't have one and the night has turned chilly.

Act in a gentlemanly fashion as if your mother were watching at all times, and you'll make any woman feel special.

Make a Memorable First Impression

Wouldn't it be nice if we all got a fair hearing from everyone we met for the first time? Of course it would. Unfortunately, that's just not how the world works. We get one shot at creating a positive image in the minds of people we're meeting for the first time. Blow it, and you usually don't get a do over.

Grooming and style are keys to starting off on the right foot. Looking sharp is in the details, and the details are what stick in people's minds.

The details start with what you wear. Even if the event is casual and doesn't call for a suit, your clothes should be meticulously clean, and chosen for how well they fit. The human eye is naturally drawn to what's out of place. You can iron that stunning blue button-down oxford perfectly, but it will be for naught if you have a nickel-sized mustard stain on the pocket. So wear clean clothes that fit right.

Your grooming follows the same rule. Dirt under your fingernails from the oil change you did this morning is going to draw more—bad—attention than the fact that you shaved.

Next focus on your approach. Shake hands firmly, look the other person in the eye, and then smile. Speak clearly, and listen intently (more than you speak). Do the toastmaster's trick of repeating the person's name after you're introduced. It's less likely to flee your memory if you've said it.

Lastly, engage. Pretend you're a journalist and you have to write an article about the person in front of you. Be polite, but ask questions. Hobbies, travel, college experiences, shared history with the host, all are fair game. Politics, religion, and sex, are not. Learn about the person and be a gentlemen and you'll leave a glowing first impression.

Ask Her Out the First Time

Don't be freaked out by a butterfly-filled stomach when you start thinking about asking that lovely lady out on a date. You are not alone. It is the rare male who is truly confident in the face of possible rejection from a member of the fairer sex.

There should be something she said or did that leads you to believe she'd actually go out with you. Does she make frequent eye contact with you across the room? Did she seek you out to chat you up? And, most important, does she lean in and touch your arm or shoulder every couple of sentences? If the answers are "yes," step to the plate, Bro, you're ready to swing for the fences.

The best way to get to asking her out on a date is to find mutual interest. Movies are a great place to start. Talk about a new release and gauge her interest. If she says something like, "I can't wait to see that one," that is the sound of opportunity's door opening for you. Suggest you see it together.

You can use the same approach with art openings (aren't you hoity toity?), car shows (no, you aren't), concerts in the park, or just about any other happening that she shows an interest in.

The beauty of this backdoor approach is that, unlike an invitation to dinner, the suggestion that you share an experience is open to interpretation. It can be as much a casual friends thing as a date. So you leave the meaning open and you both have a chance to decide where the "date" goes from there.

Play it cool, keep your head about you, and be a gentleman through and through, and this may be the first time you ask her out, but it won't be the last.

Plan the Perfect Romantic Dinner

Don't kid yourself, kid, women love to eat every bit as much as men do. They like good food, good wine, good company, and all three put together in a memorable evening. The meal that wraps all that up in a nice satin bow, and includes a killer dessert to boot, is sure to peg your score on the old heart-spinning meter.

The best romantic meal is completely unique. Reservations aren't impressive. Showing you put a lot of thought and creativity into a meal is. That creativity should start with how you dress the table. There are three must haves (well, aside from plates and silverware): candles, flowers, and a tablecloth. The candles should provide just enough light to dine by. You can do that through the size or number of candles. Two votives won't cut it, Jack.

Flowers can be anything: her favorite, classic roses, something unusual like passionflower blossoms. Just as long as they don't stand so tall as to block your view of each other. The tablecloth should always be white, and cannot be the flat sheet from your extra set. Foot the bill for a nice, white tablecloth. She'll be pleasantly shocked.

Set the table simply, with a fork for each course, but only one knife and one spoon. Wine is the lubricant of love, so you'll need some wine glasses unless you met at an AA meeting. You'll also need water glasses because hey, everyone gets thirsty. Especially when she's choked up. At how thoughtful you are.

That leaves the food. At least three courses are the baseline for a romantic dinner: salad, main course, and dessert. Extra points for an appetizer. Stick with simple fare that is easy to make, and especially anything that can be made ahead. Think shrimp cocktail, a tossed green salad with arugula, and a NY strip with a side of steamed veggies. It is within the rules of a romantic dinner to purchase the dessert. A heart-shaped double

chocolate mini cake is a good choice. A cupcake split in two will work. A plate of chocolate dipped strawberries you can feed each other is a natural. Cookies out of the box, are not.

If you're feeling a little more adventurous, you can take the whole show on the road. Pack the meal up in a box (use Sterno to warm what you need to warm) and bring along a card table and folding chairs if necessary. The beach is a classic favorite, but not much good in the winter. A favorite picnic ground with a stunning view of the mountains could be another winner. Find the right place, put a little effort in, and you'll be eating kisses for dessert.

Plan the Perfect First Date

There are those moments when the stars align, Cupid is your best friend, and you actually trip upon that woman who is quite obviously meant to be the center of your universe. At those moments, you need a first date that will knock her off her pins and make her see you as soul mate.

The best dates are the most memorable, which doesn't necessarily mean the most expensive. Yeah, every woman would love a dinner at the ritziest restaurant in town, but that's setting the bar high, and it doesn't do much to show how original, clever, and creative you are.

Look for an interest on her Facebook page, in talking to her, or even in the photos she has plastered in her cubicle. If she's a sports fanatic—lucky you—find front row tickets to her favorite team or create a night around a college, minor league or even high school game.

On the same note, stay away from skill-based endeavors. You'll know soon enough if she wants to learn Tae Kwon Do; a first date is no place for lessons.

The ideal date gives you time sitting next to each other. Side-by-side seating creates a lot of opportunities for incidental contact that you won't get sitting across from each other. Contact leads to comfort with each other. Follow?

Whatever the date is, it should provide some entertainment so that you don't have to interact the entire date, but it should also provide a chance to talk one-on-one. Think wine-and-cheese picnic before a concert in the park. Now you're getting the idea.

And watch your clock, loverboy. A date shouldn't run so long that she's exhausted by the end of it. The cardinal rule in dating, as in so much of life, is always leave her wanting more.

Meet Her Parents

You don't just date a woman. If all goes right and things progress like they should, you eventually date her parents. The first time you meet the folks affects how you'll interact for the rest of time, and how fully you'll be accepted into their little circle.

You have total power over how even the most critical parents view you. It's simply a matter of a charm offensive. That starts with proper prior preparation. Get all the information you can from your girlfriend. This information will be invaluable to you, so pay close attention. Preparation also includes coming up with some pat answers to common questions like, "So what are your intentions?" Be as honest as possible while still being as vague as possible. Spend some time on those answers; they will be your best friends.

Every charm offensive has a dress code and yours is business casual. A suit screams you're trying too hard, while your ripped Metallica T-shirt says you're not trying at all. Pressed trousers, a button down shirt, and a nice blazer work every time.

Bring a gift. If her parents are drinkers, wine works well. If not, flowers in a vase. Look both of her parents in the eye when you're being introduced, and shake hands firmly.

Conversation should be no problem. Focus on their interests and ask about your girlfriend's childhood. Impress them with how you treat her (see chivalry, page 212). Don't fawn on her or them, but be solicitous. Compliment the food if there is any, compliment the house unless it's a trailer on cinderblocks, and get out as quickly as possible. Thank them for their hospitality and leave the door open by telling them you hope to see them soon. Shake hands with dad, and if mom makes the gesture, give her a hug.

The very word sends chills down many men's spines. It's the romantic equivalent of diving off a cliff into water whose depth is a mystery. It's some scary stuff.

But the right woman is the right woman and sooner or later, she's going to want to see some metal and mineral on her finger as a sign you're a serious man.

When that time comes, she should have an inkling, but the actual moment should be a surprise. You are creating one of the most memorable moments that either of you will ever experience (and hopefully the only time either of you will ever experience it). Do it right.

Choose a location that is either incredibly spectacular, purely nostalgic, or both. If she's an out-loud type of person, on bended knee in a crowded restaurant will be fine. If she's the quieter type, the top of your favorite mountain might be better. The ice rink where you went for your first date? In the middle of Paris? At your favorite ice cream parlor? All cool locales. It's just got to have meaning and impact.

Same goes for when. Pop the question in the middle of a busy workday, and you're creating more chaos where there is already chaos. The end of a wonderful date night is a better choice.

When it comes to actually popping the question, the great and unimpeachable first rule is to know that she will say yes. If you're not absolutely certain, don't ask, pal. That's one soul-crushing you don't want to endure. But if you're a confident lad, propose in a classic way, on bended knee. Eschew the radio DJ proposal, or the skywritten proposal. This is one of the most intimate, life changing moments two people can share; it's better not to turn it into a 15-second ad spot.

Pick a Diamond

Choosing a rock to hang off someone's finger for time immemorial may seem daunting, but it isn't. First, pick a shape: emerald (rectangular and blocky), marquise (a football), pear, oval, or the most popular: brilliant cut (round with a tapered base). Go with the one she likes the best.

Diamonds are judged by four Cs: color, cut, clarity, and carats. The best diamonds have a pure, clear color, the worst are noticeably yellow. Check the color against a glossy, bright white piece of paper. Cut is the faceting of the diamond, which determines how much it sparkles.

Clarity is a measure of imperfections in the diamond's structure of the diamond. Judge your diamond under the magnifying glass of a jeweler's loop. If you can't pick out the imperfections that way, she'll never see them either. Carat equals size. Size matters, but better a beautiful, wildly sparkling clear diamond, than a huge, yellow eyesore.